EASYKAYAKER
A guide to laid-back paddling

Gary Backlund
Paul Grey

Greyswan Publications
Vancouver Island, British Columbia

An order form is available at the back of this book.

National Library of Canada Cataloguing in Publication Data

Backlund, Gary, 1951-
Easykayaker : a guide to laid-back paddling

Includes bibliographical references and index.
ISBN 0-9687858-1-6

1. Sea kayaking—British Columbia—Gulf Islands—Guidebooks.
2. Sea kayaking—British Columbia—Barkley Sound—Guidebooks.
3. Sea kayaking—British Columbia—Nootka Sound—Guidebooks.
4. Gulf Islands (B.C.)—Guidebooks. 5. Barkley Sound (B.C.)—Guide-books. 6. Nootka Sound (B.C.)—Guidebooks.
I. Grey, Paul, 1951-
II. Title.
GV776.15.B7B32 2001   797.1'224'097112   C2001-900149-5

Printed by Friesens Corporation
One Printers Way
Altona, Manitoba, Canada   R0G 0B0
Printed in Canada.

Cover design by Paul Grey and Gary Backlund
Front and back cover photos by Marina Sacht

Greyswan Publications   Easykayaker
3285 Roper Road   http://www.easykayaker.com
Ladysmith, BC V9G 1C4   ekayaker@island.net
Canada

Distributed and marketed by Wave Publications Cooperative

Acknowledgements

From the first stroke of the paddle to the last stroke of the pen it's been quite an experience. Support from many people made this long journey possible ~ from our first paddle to writing and publishing *Easykayaker*.

We would like to first thank our wives, **Teesh Backlund** and **Imelda Grey** for their encouragement and Teesh for her many hours of proofing and editing. We'd like to thank our children **Katherine Backlund** and **Jordan Grey** for their contributions to *"Kayaking with kids."*

We would like to thank **Celia Norris** for her proofing and critiquing of *Easykayaker*.

If it wasn't for the following people teaching us about kayaking, opening our eyes to issues facing paddlesports, and supplying us with technical information, this book may never have been written.

Bud Bell of Sealegs Kayak & Marine Adventures

Gillian Butler and **Brian Collen** of Pacific Northwest Expeditions

Kim Crosby of Wildheart Adventures

Melanie Graham of the Ladysmith Paddlers Club

Mark Hall of Azul Kayaks

Cliff Hermann of Seadog Sailing & Kayaking Adventures

John Surtees of Seaward Kayaks

Thank you all, it's because of people like you that Vancouver Island sea kayaking is what it is today.

A special credit goes to **Marina Sacht**, publisher and editor of Ladysmith's *Take 5 Magazine*, for our front and rear cover photos.

Last but not least, thanks to all our paddling partners that shared the journey, many of whom are mentioned in the book.

Happy paddling,

Gary Backlund
Paul Grey

Contents

Section 6—Kayaking With Kids

Section 7—With a Little Help From Your Commercial Friends

Section 8—The Most Popular Kayaking Area in the World

Section 9—Other Vancouver Island Paddles

Bibliography and Suggested Reading 186

Index 187

Wishful thinking...

Section 1—Easykayaker

About the book

Paul and Gary had been kayaking the local waters of Vancouver Island for several years and during a spring morning paddle around Kuper Island, an idea hit them and washed over them like a wave. Actually it was two ideas, but they were similar thoughts.

They had taken the ferry to Thetis Island and driven to a launch site about halfway up the canal between Telegraph Harbour and Clam Bay (see section on Thetis launches). The weather was great, there was no wind and paddling was idyllic (although that would change later in the day).

As they paddled out of Telegraph Harbour and rounded the corner to head down the western shore of Kuper Island, the ideas seemed to hit them both at once. Gary's idea was to write a kayaking book and Paul's idea was to create a kayaking website. As they paddled along discussing the ideas, it turned out that the book and website concepts were very similar as far as purpose, content and target readers. Paul and Gary had read most of the local paddling books and their idea was to do something different.

Thus *Easykayaker* the book and www.easykayaker.com were born. The "easy" concept was to apply to all aspects. They would list easy-to-use launch sites, easy-to-paddle trips and the book would be easy reading. The website would be easy to navigate and it would also be a listing of all Vancouver Island kayaking related businesses, so people could find equipment, kayaking rentals, lodging, and tour guides plus weather, tides and much more no matter where on Vancouver Island they were planning to paddle.

The target group would be people like Paul and Gary who were baby-boomers and/or families that paddled with their children. They would be mostly day paddlers and be at the beginner or intermediate level as kayakers. Paul and Gary did some research with the BC Ministry of Tourism, BC Parks and Parks Canada. It turned out that Paul and Gary's favourite paddling area, the Gulf Islands, was the world's most popular paddling area. They also found out that baby-boomers (ages 35 – 50) were the fastest growing segment of kayakers and that just over 70% of all BC ocean kayakers class themselves as beginner to intermediate level kayakers (averaging four years of kayaking experience). It also appears that about half the kayaking person hours in BC is for day paddles and the other half for overnight trips.

Easykayaker the book will give you, the kayaker, basic information about launch sites and enjoyable paddling routes, kayaking safety, equipment, weather, tides and currents. For the beginner there's a section on tips and for the kayak buyer there's a section on buying new and used kayaks. There's even a section on kayak care, maintenance and repair for those that own their own boats.

Easykayaker is also for those who want to rent kayaks, use motherships/ sisterships or go on guided trips. There are sections explaining the industry norms and what to look for and expect when dealing with the commercial segment of the local kayaking industry.

Although *Easykayaker* has focused mainly on the Gulf Islands and eastern Vancouver Island, some other popular Vancouver Island paddling locations have been included along with kayaking camping information and kayaking etiquette.

Lastly, there's a section written for kayaking with kids, written by both parents and their kids. It includes perspectives from both view points (often at each end of the towline), choosing the right boat for kayaking with kids, and tips from parents and kids on how to make sure the experience is a whole lot of fun.

If you kayak in Vancouver Island waters or want to, *Easykayaker* should be a wonderful resource, enjoyable reading and a good motivational boost to get out there and do some kayaking!

Gary's introduction to kayaking

The first time I paddled a kayak was a white knuckled experience, yet later that day I would place an order to purchase my first ocean-touring kayak. I guess I should back up a bit and explain the circumstances.

My wife, daughter and I had recently completed a hair-raising trip by freight canoe down Green (McNeill) River to the Skeena River and then down the Skeena to a piece of wilderness we own at Boneyard Creek. The Skeena is tidal for sixty miles up river and three miles wide where we were paddling. Tide changes of twenty feet combined with an opposing wind off the Inside Passage created some less than desirable conditions. We had bought the ideal canoe for this trip, a Sea Clipper ocean-going freighter. With my twenty years' experience canoeing rivers, lakes and ocean, we felt comfortable with this trip.

We were warned by many while researching our Skeena trip that this portion of the river was dangerous. On the last day of our trip while heading back up the river, we passed a fish boat setting their net and when we jokingly asked if this was the way to Terrace, we were warned yet again. We had left with the tide at dawn, but before we could reach Mowitch Point the tide turned against us and we were stuck in the foggy drizzle unable to paddle against the raging current coming around the point.

Eventually the current slowed. The occasional trees, complete with stumps, that had been racing by were now coming by quite slowly. The three of us hopped in the canoe and set off around the point. We knew if we could just clear the point, we could catch back-eddies from there on until the tide changed in our favour. We did quite well at first but our forward motion slowed to a stop just as our objective came into view. We gave it all we had, but to no avail. We quickly turned around and returned to our waiting place on the west side of Mowitch Point. We arrived to find fresh wolf tracks at our waiting place.

A half-hour later was slack tide, the sun came out and the slight wind abated. We got back into the canoe and the rest of our trip home was great. Even so, after that, the canoe went into one of our storage sheds and I didn't paddle again until my first time in a kayak, about seven months later.

I first met Kim by doing an energy audit of his home. After the audit he showed me his ocean-touring kayaks. Compared to my canoe these things looked like sport-class racecars. They certainly didn't look as seaworthy as my wide flat-bottomed canoe (which handled like a dump truck), nor did they look like they would stay easily upright. Kim, a great salesperson and adventure outfitter, soon had me wanting to try out a kayak.

Kim phoned one early March day and said he would be ordering some kayaks. Did I want to go for a test paddle tomorrow to see if I wanted to order one? I agreed, but that night a storm moved in with high winds and heavy rain. By morning the storm had blown itself out but the seas were still angry. I phone him to see if he was canceling, but to my surprise he said no.

I drove to Kim's house, helped him load gear and two kayaks onto his van and headed to the boat ramp at Cedar-by-the-Sea. There were small waves breaking as he gave me some quick instructions and we launched. As we paddled out toward Round Island I could feel and see the tidal currents caused by nearby Dodd Narrows. The angry seas reminded me of the waves and whitecaps of our trip on the Skeena.

I was white knuckled and yet amazed at how I felt in this boat. I didn't feel like I was in a boat on the water. I felt like I was in the water and that the boat was part of me. The power and control that I had was incredible! As we rounded Round Island (no pun intended), we were broadsided by waves. The knuckles got whiter, but Kim explained how stable we were and I relaxed somewhat, although I occasionally had water flowing over my decks and one wave even hit me hard enough to submerge my arm from the elbow down.

We had a mini surf landing back at the boat ramp. Kim landed first and then helped me. I was happy to be out of those water conditions, but boy was I impressed with this type of paddling craft. That day I gave Kim the go-ahead to order me an ocean-touring kayak.

Contrary to the above, I'm not a thrill seeker and really prefer to paddle glassy, calm water with the occasional wave caused by a passing boat. Lakes and rivers somehow don't interest me like the saltwater does. I love the tides, the wildlife, the clear water and marine life. The ever-changing coastline, reefs, inlets, beaches, cliffs, rock formations, islets and islands are like works of art as I paddle along. Never have I felt a greater appreciation for the marvels of nature than when paddling a kayak.

I can see why the sport is growing at a 20% rate each year. It provides an opportunity to pursue environmental, outdoor and fitness interests without requiring heavy physical exercise or advanced activity skill levels. This and other types of "soft adventure" tourism are growing rapidly, and not only in British Columbia. Soft adventure refers to travel or activities, which involve mild exertion, are located in visibly attractive areas and include opportunity for learning. I hope that *Easykayaker* enhances some of your soft adventures while paddling our local waters.

Gary Backlund

Paul's introduction to kayaking

Ocean kayaking! Close your eyes for a moment and say, "Ocean Kayaking," slowly. Do your thoughts wander to light, rolling swells with a warm, summer breeze blowing across your bow or do you imagine yourself paddling quietly along a shore, early evening, as you watch shadows dance on the water?

I'm sure each reader has a different vision and a different reason to ocean kayak. Each year I discover new rocky shores, small inlets, or a log made just for me on a desolate beach. It's fun to stop for lunch on a West Coast ocean beach with a thousand tide-swept shells embedded in the coarse sand or endure a chilly, weekend autumn day only to see river otters playfully skipping across the waves. The sea kayak has special properties that kindle one's spirit. It quickly takes you from your workplace of tools and talk to a typically quiet location with reflective waters and the cry of eagles. It passes fisherman repairing their nets as you slip by unnoticed. It catches wildlife unexpectedly like a sea lion rising between your boats with a look of surprise on its face. The sea kayak battles tide and wind and suffers an occasional scratch across its hull from an unsuspecting rock hidden by seaweed. It treats you so well it should be waxed or scrubbed at least once a year with a little affection!

I first paddled with Gary, the co-author, along Thetis Island, on a gray, cloudy day in his double kayak. Apparently, I was a pretty good paddler not a thrasher, a water splasher or one who took long sustained breaks (Gary was in the stern watching me). I met the standards of being a good 'Easykayaker'—one who enjoys casual days paddling along the rocky shores of British Columbia. From there kayaking became part of my life. I soon bought a secondhand, plastic Storm kayak made by Current Designs. It stood two years of time until I bought a fibreglass Solstice GTS (high volume) that carried slightly more gear than its sister design. The Solstice, a boat with good initial and excellent secondary stability, smoothly cuts through the water. It's a few pounds lighter than my Storm and enables me to easily handle packing it by myself onto my car.

I've been on dozens of trips with family, friends, and paddling partners since that first day. I've discovered moonlight paddles or howls, crabbing by kayak, and observing fireworks by water on a holiday weekend. One day I'd like to paddle a new coastline in a different country, but for now I still have at least a thousand new places to go along Vancouver Island shores.

Paul Grey

Gary and Paul out for a Christmas paddle

Section 2—Kayak Safety

Basic safety for kayaking

Safety on the water involves knowing and interpreting marine conditions. Possessing the basic safety equipment and learning self-rescue is paramount to kayaking safety. With that said, kayaking is a safe water sport. Kayaks are very stable, much more so than canoes and most other boats under 20 feet in length. The following are some basic safety guidelines.

1. Check the marine conditions for your area either from a marine radio forecast, by phoning the local marine weather office, and/or checking through Internet (go to the Weather link and choose Marine at www.easykayaker.com). Remember the winds vary considerably in the Strait of Georgia. The marine weather radio station (Coastguard) gives wind and sea conditions for specific sites such as Saturna Island, Ballenas Island, Entrance Island and Strait of Georgia. Unfortunately, these sites are not within much of the area covered by our Easykayaker launch locations. However, these reference sites do surround our area but they are more exposed. Wind and sea conditions will almost always be slightly more favourable than what is reported for Saturna Island, Ballenas Island, Entrance Island and Strait of Georgia.

2. Know the tides! Most marine-related stores offer free tide guides. An official set of tide and currents from Fisheries and Oceans Canada can also be purchased from many marine suppliers for about $7.95. Tide information is also available from the Reference Page at www.easykayaker.com. Tides may determine your launch site and destination. Tides also cause currents. Determine the flood and ebb for the area where you are planning on paddling. Remembering flood is the tide rising and ebbing is the tide lowering. The arrow on the chart with "feathers" on one side is the flood and the arrow without feathers is the ebb. If the current speed is over 1 knot, it will be shown with the arrows.

3. Have the proper marine chart for the area you will be paddling and carry a compass. The chart will indicate the strength of ebbing and

flooding currents. You can travel about 3 to 4 knots per hour in your kayak. Paddling against a 3 knot current is not fun. Although Vancouver Island's east coast seldom has fog, having a compass can be important if it does get foggy or dark. Marine charts are available from many marine stores and specialty marine chart shops. Three marine charts cover our first 16 launches on the East Coast of Vancouver Island. Check our www.easykayaker.com Reference Page for more details.

4.   Check the wind direction compared to tide flow. If tide and wind are traveling the same direction, water conditions are often somewhat calm. When the wind is traveling against the tidal current, waves will be created.

5.   Attach your paddle to the kayak with a paddle leash. (Unless you are an experienced kayaker.)

6.   Take at least one litre of water for a day's kayaking and a snack. Have the water accessible while paddling. It's too easy to get dehydrated, which can cause problems. Up to three litres are recommended for warm days.

7.   Have at least the basic safety equipment for a day's paddling that is required by the Coastal Regulations plus one spare paddle per group (see Coastal Regulations below). A small first aid kit, toilet paper, extra warm clothes and other items are also recommended.

8.   Stay with your group. Always kayak with at least one other person. Stay within calling or whistle blowing distance of each other. A two-person rescue is much easier than a self-rescue. Lone kayaks are hard for other boaters to see. By staying in a group, other boats are less likely to run into you and large boats have a better chance of seeing a group of kayaks on their radar. There are 'Rules of the Road' which are also called 'Collision Regulations'.

9.   Know how to perform a self-rescue and an assisted rescue. You should know how to wet-exit from your kayak in case you capsize and how to use a paddle float to do a self-rescue / wet-entry. Wet-exiting is scary to most people, but it is very easy. The paddle float is designed for the paddle to slip into it (practice this so you know where it fits). Once one end of a paddle is in the float, the other end is pushed under the cords that are crisscrossed behind your cockpit. At Easykayaker we strongly recommend you take some basic training on self and assisted rescue and practice these techniques in the warm waters of a lake or pool with a partner. Do not expect to be able to do an Eskimo roll, as this is an advanced technique, however learning to brace with your paddle is not difficult and well worth practicing.

10. File a float plan. Let someone know where you're going paddling and approximately when you will return.

Coastal Regulations for kayaking

The safe boating regulations for kayaks under and over 6 metres in length can be found at this website: www.ccg-gcc.gc.ca/obs-bsn/sbg-gsn/main.htm. Choose kayaks under the Safe Boating heading. For your convenience the information for kayaks under 6 metres is included below:

- one Canadian-approved personal flotation device or lifejacket of appropriate size for each person on board
- one buoyant heaving line of not less than 15 m in length
- one manual propelling device (paddle) or an anchor with not less than 15 m of cable, rope or chain in any combination
- one bailer or manual water pump fitted with or accompanied by sufficient hose to enable a person to pump over the vessel's side
- one sound signaling device or appliance (usually a whistle attached to your lifejacket or an air horn)
- navigation lights that meet applicable standards if the craft is to be operated after sunset, before sunrise or in periods of restricted visibility

Note: many double kayaks are over 20 feet (6 metres) in length and require the above equipment plus flares.

Rescue techniques

If you venture away from the sandy shore, you'd better know how to get back into your kayak from the water. Capsizing is always a possibility when in a boat no matter what size it is. Capsizing from a kayak is called a "wet-exit." Getting back in from the water is called a "wet-entry." Learning the wet-exit is straightforward, the only things you need to know is how to release your sprayskirt if it doesn't self-release and to stay with the boat. Your legs virtually fall out of the kayak during a wet-exit once it's upside down.

A wet-entry, on the other hand, is not easy unless you know the techniques and have practiced them. If the seas are rough it may not be easy even for the experienced. Before we talk about types of wet-entries and equipment needed, location is important. You won't have the opportunity to choose the spot for your accidental capsize, but you are able to choose where not to capsize by not paddling there. So when conditions are rough keep your paddling route away from rocky shores and when possible try to paddle along beaches that provide nice landings. Only twice have I had to deal with an inexperienced paddler wet-exiting and both times I had kept our paddling route in safe areas where I could pull the wet kayaker to shore quickly instead of bothering with a wet-entry. It would have been a nightmare to try and rescue an inexperienced paddler being pounded into the rocks by the surf.

There are two main methods of rescues, self-rescue and assisted rescue. The assisted rescue is the easiest and the preferred method as long as the person in the water doesn't do something stupid and put you both in the water. Don't go kayaking without learning these techniques from either a kayaking course or from an experience kayaker. I spoke to one beginning kayaker who went kayaking off the West Coast of Vancouver Island by himself and capsized. The current carried him away from the beach and he spent forty minutes trying to do a wet-entry (he didn't know how) before he was rescued by a powerboat.

Let's start with the self-rescue technique. Your first requirement is to paddle without much on the deck of the kayak that will get in the way of a rescue. Once you have capsized you must right the kayak and in doing so, try to remove as much water as possible. At the same time don't loose your paddle (a paddle leash is recommended for beginners).

Attach your paddle float to the blade of the paddle, slide the other blade on the kayak under the shock cords behind the cockpit. You now have an outrigger for stabilization (see photos). Next, with your head pointed toward the rudder, place one hand on the paddle shaft and the other hand on the far side of the cockpit coaming, and climb up so your chest comes onto the rear deck. Swing your legs into the cockpit. You will now be partly in the cockpit and staring at the rudder with the paddle blade under your chest or stomach. Rotate your body around so that you're right side up and finish sliding into the cockpit. Now you need to get the rest of the water out of your kayak, retrieve your paddle from behind you and detach your paddle float. And you get to do this in waves how high? It's fairly simple to do in

a swimming pool. Real life conditions can be something else. One last note, for some of us, crawling up on the back deck isn't easy with a PFD on. One solution is to carry a 10-foot rope tied into a loop. Slip this loop over the cockpit lip (coaming) and let it extend into the water as a stirrup. It makes climbing back in much easier.

Assisted rescue starts out the same way. Instead of a paddle float being used as an outrigger, you will have your boat steadied by another kayaker that is still dry and afloat in their kayak. The first thing that happens is that the person in the water rights their boat and positions it in a T-formation with the other kayak such that their bow is even with the dry person's lap.

The person in the water pushes down on the rudder area and the dry person lifts the bow onto their lap. At this point both people turn the kayak upside down to remove the water from the cockpit (see photo). Take note that this is not a maneuver to try with a fully loaded kayak.

The kayak is righted, slid off the dry kayaker's lap and turned facing the opposite direction of the first kayak. Now you should have two kayaks side by side facing opposite directions. The dry kayaker reaches over with both hands and grabs both sides of the cockpit coaming a little forward to the centre of the cockpit opening. This makes both boats very stable and the wet kayaker can crawl up on the rear deck similar to a self-rescue (but

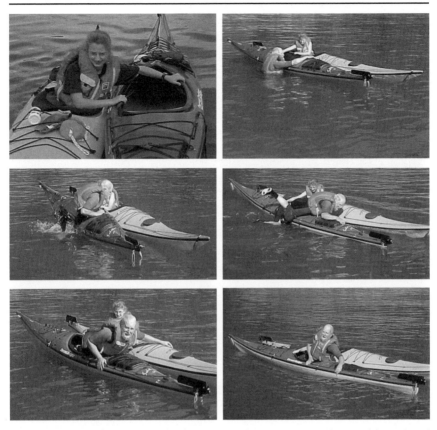

without the outrigger), slide in and swivel. There's a variation to this assisted rescue where the wet kayaker enters from the other side by crawling over the dry kayaker's boat to get into their own boat.

Once you have learned these rescue techniques, practice them. It's hard on your chest and stomach and it scratches boats, but it can be lifesaving. If possible find a beach on a warm sunny day with some wave action and try the techniques in more realistic conditions.

Tips for novice kayakers

Kayaking is very safe and suitable for ages from 8 to 98. Most kayaking accidents happen to novice and expert level kayakers. The novice can run into problems from being inexperienced and the experts tend to push the envelope too far. Here are some very basic tips:

- Choose a Canadian-approved life jacket that fits you well (matches your weight and size). The proper term for lifejacket is "personal flotation device" (PFD). It may not save your life, but it will keep you afloat. The PFD should be a colour that is highly visible and ideally your kayak should also be a highly visible colour. Reflective tape on your PFD and paddles add to your safety

- For your first few outings, go with an experienced and knowledgeable kayaker who can teach you the basics of paddling including rescue (wet-entry). This may be a friend, adventure guide or kayaking instructor
- Ask questions about the kayaks. Are my pedals set correctly? What's the best way to get in? How do I use the safety equipment?
- Make sure your paddle is attached by cord to the kayak (recommended for beginners)
- Check the kayak seat. Some are uncomfortable. Add some thin foam if needed for comfort and try adjusting the seat back. Caution: by raising the seat one-inch with a cushion, you can halve the stability of some touring kayaks
- Minimize the amount of deck cargo. Deck cargo interferes with wind, righting a capsized boat and also makes wet-entry difficult

Equipment for a kayak day trip

The trip will be more enjoyable if it is well planned. Some of the following items are overkill for a two-hour summer paddle, but makes sense if you are going out for a six-hour January paddle.

- Kayak Equipment: In a kayak under 6 metres in length you should have basic equipment for a day's paddle. This equipment includes: a life jacket (PFD), a sprayskirt, a pump or bailer (can), sponge, paddle, a whistle, a paddle float, a spare paddle (one per group), and a buoyant heaving line
- Navigation: You should have a compass, charts for the area (and waterproof bag if charts aren't laminated), and Tide and Current Tables. Optional is a GPS unit (great in the fog!) if you know how to properly use one
- Safety: Include a towline (unless the buoyant heaving line is suitable for towing), duct tape, first aid kit, foil survival blanket, waterproof matches, and kayak repair kit (see June/July issue Wavelength magazine, 1999). For summertime day trips, the kayak repair kit can consist of a partial roll of duct tape. You may want to include flares, and a weather or VHF radio

- Gear: Rain gear (preferably light) or paddling jacket, cap or sun hat, paddling boots (wet suit booties) or good sandals, quick-drying shorts, sunscreen, sunglasses, flashlight and extra batteries (if paddling in the evening), sunglasses, toilet paper, water bottles (up to 3 litres per day) and paddling gloves are all extras that you may want along. During the cool part of the year, long underwear (preferably polypropylene) and a warm change of clothes are advised. Instead of booties or sandals, some people use gumboots in the wintertime
- Additional Optional Items: Crab trap, knife, food, firestarter, fishing gear (and license), camera, binoculars, and cell phone are additional items that some paddlers include. Use common sense, don't drag out more gear than necessary for your paddle, but be prepared if you plan to paddle in an isolated area.

Tides, currents and charts

Tides

Tide predictions for East Vancouver Island and the Gulf Islands are available in *Tide and Current Tables, Vol. 5*, published yearly by the Canadian Hydrographic Society. An hour needs to be added from April to October for Pacific Daylight Time. Knowing the tides ahead of time or having a tide table booklet along for reference during your paddle can help you make prudent plans and decisions along the way relating to many aspects of your trip. Here are a few suggestions based on tide levels.

- launching and landing boats during a mid to high tide is often preferable (shorter carrying distances)
- traveling up the mouth of a river can often be accomplished during a high tide
- exploring inlets, lagoons, small passages, and between islands during a slack or higher tide may become possible
- tying your boat up because the tide will soon be higher (we've heard at least one story of a kayak floating away in the night!)
- better beachcombing and more beach area at low tides
- knowing how high the tide will come up overnight while camping on the beach can be very important when choosing a tent site
- knowing the tidal flow will help you predict currents in order to paddle with instead of against them

A tide table booklet will set you back less than $10. Fortunately, there are local advertisers that produce free tidetable booklets. The free ones predict tides only in feet and not in metres, but that's probably not an issue with most people. The free ones are also corrected for daylight savings time, which caused a problem for one person we know that missed slack tide by an hour and therefore couldn't beat the current through Gabriola Passage. Because they are free and small, we always keep one in a ziplock bag in the back pocket of our PFDs.

The Internet is also a great way of getting tide information for any location on the West Coast of BC. The Easykayaker website has links under the Reference Tables section and it also lists which tidal reference points to use for looking up tides for each area.

Currents

A normal cruising speed for a kayak is around 4 knots (7 km/hr). Gary and I occasionally paddle with a GPS (Global Positioning System) and have noted speeds of up to 5 knots (9 km/hr)—a little wind and current are very helpful! Several of the passes in the Gulf Islands can flow at more than 5 knots (Dodd Narrows can flow at close to 10 knots!), making it impossible to paddle against, and very dangerous to paddle with. No one wants to experience being drawn into a 10 metre wide whirlpool in a kayak! Subsequently, you must enter a pass during a slack water time, which is often when the tide is changing direction. Usually, a reasonable window of time is open for you to make it through the passageway. Many power and sailboats unfortunately will also choose this time.

The *Tide and Current Tables* provide slack water times and maximum flow times in relation to a Reference Station and to a Secondary Station. The Secondary Stations have adjusted times and current speeds that apply to a more specific area.

Some passages in the northern Gulf Islands that require advanced kayaking skills and proper timing are Dodd Narrows (between Vancouver Island and Mudge Island), Gabriola Passage (between Gabriola Island and Valdes Island), Porlier Pass (between Valdes Island and Galiano Island), Active Pass (between Galiano Island and Mayne Island) and the passes between Mayne and Saturna Islands.

Paddlers should also use care and proper timing when passing through False Narrows (between Mudge Island and Gabriola Island). You will also want to go with the current through much of Sansum Narrows. Most of the other passes don't drain large bodies of water, so there will be some current flows but they won't be too strong. A couple of examples are the passes between North & South Pender Islands and between Thetis and Kuper Islands.

The waters outside some of the fast moving passes can be affected for quite a distance. Paddling too close to the mouths of these passages can cause you to be sucked into the passage if the current is flowing away from you.

The current in Porlier Pass flows all the way to Kuper Island and down Houstoun Passage on a strong ebb tide. These currents are only a problem if you're paddling toward them. Fortunately, on a flood tide, currents from Porlier Pass do not affect Houstoun Passage in the Kuper Island area.

With four tides happening over an approximate twenty-five hour period, it's likely you will experience a flooding or ebbing tide or both during your paddle. A combination of a 1 to 3 knot current and a headwind can turn the joy of gliding easily through the water into work. On one of our trips, Gary and I paddled northeast through Maple Bay with its light rippling waves, past Arbutus Point into Sansum Narrows and suddenly met adverse conditions. A tidal rip, higher winds, and a disturbed sea fed by rebounding waves, rocked our boats in a variety of directions. Other trips through False Narrows and Gabriola Passage gave us little trouble with wind, but the currents contained back eddies which often made steering interesting.

Although currents are directly related to tides, there isn't a direct correlation. The time of slack tide and slack water often differ by 30 to 60 minutes. One of the best ways to know what the current will be doing is to use the *Current Atlas – Juan de Fuca to Strait of Georgia*, ISBN 0-660-52380-9, produced by the Canadian Hydrographic Service, Department of Fisheries and Oceans. This book will cost about $25. The book consists of 94 charts showing tidal current flows for the area from Campbell River to Port Angeles.

This book can be used year after year if you have a set of Murray's tables for the current year. Murray's tables cost about $8. By looking up each hour you will be paddling, you can predict currents for not just the passes and narrows but for your entire paddling route. Each hour references one of the 94 charts and that chart will give you the flows for that hour.

Navigational Charts
The different paddles described in this book are accompanied with chart numbers. Some magazine outlets, kayak and marine shops provide an overview of Canadian Hydrographic Service charts and you can purchase a chart specific to the area you will be paddling. A more comprehensive atlas of charts is also available (Chart No. 3313 costs around ninety-five dollars). The spiral bound atlas, large and cumbersome for kayakers, is best kept in large ziploc bags or marine plastic chart bags with charts folded

in four. A laminated chart can be tucked under the shock cords just forward of your cockpit.

Marine charts for much of this area are at a scale of 1:40,000 although some are at 1:20,000 and some are at 1:80,000. The 1:40,000 scale is ideal for kayaking. One inch equals one kilometre on the charts at this scale. As we normally travel at about 7 km/hr, it's easy to predict paddling times and crossing times if winds and currents don't play too large a factor. Usually the chart (if the scale is 1:40,000) can be folded to fit the chart bag so that one day's paddling can be covered without having to refold the chart.

The charts contain useful information including tidal flows, which are represented by arrows. The "feathered" arrow represents the current during flood tides and the unfeathered arrow represents currents during ebbing tides. Fisheries and Oceans also publish a booklet called *Symbols, Abbreviations and Terms,* which sells for about $6. This booklet helps you interpret all the symbols and notes on marine charts including the type of shoreline and beach.

If you plan on traveling any real distance, between multiple islands or in the fog, having a marine chart of that area is a wise idea. Knowing how to use it is also important and requires practice. Even with each paddler having a chart, we don't always agree as to where we are. At those times we are usually sitting rafted together in our kayaks floating in some cove, but where in the heck are we according to this chart? Yes, these moments do happen…

Marine winds and weather

Our typical day trips begin with quick calls the evening before. Gary often has checked the marine weather forecast and I do a quick check at the Weather Office on the Internet. The next morning we're both looking out the windows and checking the cloud type and observable effects (refer to Beaufort scale). Gary has a view to Ladysmith Harbour and I can only see the towering trees around my house. All in all, we want to hear the marine broadcast indicate that our chosen area of kayaking has moderate winds or less. While a nice, warm sun is a preferable choice of day, an overcast day is suitable too.

A novice to intermediate kayaker to the Strait of Georgia and Gulf Islands armed with a reasonable knowledge of general areas, basic equipment, sources of weather information including wind speeds and technical terms, a proper chart (directions, hazards, currents), and a compass will be able to plan a successful outing. Winds in the Strait of Georgia are generally predictable and conform to regular patterns. In the Gulf Islands, the winds are quite unpredictable. Exposure to possible wind squalls, wind directions, and other factors requires a kayaker to listen to or read a weather report before they launch. As a rule of thumb, Gary and I base the direction and length of our trip on what the weather report has to say.

Every paddler has a comfort level. That level often changes as experience grows. After paddling heavy seas, a person realizes that kayaks are incredibly stable watercrafts. When you see a beginning kayaker white-knuckled in a little chop, it's because they've exceeded their comfort level. Even to some of us with higher comfort levels, rough water is not as enjoyable as beautiful glassy conditions where one can relax more and focus their attention on the scenery.

Gary and I commonly paddle into the winds on the first leg of our paddle and ride the wind and waves back on the return trip, on occasion though, the winds have reversed direction on us! Paying attention to observable effects (listed on the Beaufort scale below) such as flags extending themselves or long unbreaking waves, also help in your assessment of weather conditions. A compilation of weather sources can be found on Easykayaker's web site.

The Canadian Coastguard and Environment Canada provide around-the-clock marine forecasts for East Vancouver Island and the Gulf Islands. As well marine forecasts can be found through the 'Weather Office' on the Internet (www.weatheroffice.com). The forecasts are a synopsis of weather systems that will most likely influence local waters. Knowledge of technical or common terms used on the broadcasts can be very helpful. Wind orientation is given as to the direction the wind is coming from. In other words, a southeast wind is blowing from the southeast toward the northwest.

Wind speed is measured in knots

light   0 – 10 knots
moderate   11 – 19 knots
strong   20 – 33 knots

Wave heights are represented by metres. The most frequent warning on the broadcasts are 'small craft warnings'. This common saying really means that a strong wind is expected.

Weather Radio Canada (Environment Canada) broadcasts marine weather forecasts at frequencies from 162.40 to 162.55 and Canadian Coast Guard at 161.65. Gary has a radio scanner in his home and has programmed it with these frequencies. We also have an inexpensive 7 channel Radio Shack Weatheradio, which fits nicely in a ziplock sandwich bag and travels with us on longer trips. Many people have VHF radios, which are also good for receiving marine weather broadcasts.

When camping, you can usually see fellow kayakers at their campsite listening to their radios first thing in the morning. Ironically, the Radio Shack unit, which costs about $40, often gets better reception than radios that cost many times more. The best radio to have if you can afford it is a VHF radio as it can be used to call for help in an emergency or to contact other boats. We recently purchased a handheld waterproof VHF radio for $400 plus taxes. Expensive, but if it saves a life it's more than worth it. A cell phone will also work for most areas locally if you need to make a call. However in some areas like Nootka Sound, cell phones don't have coverage.

Back to weather forecasts. Receiving the forecast is one thing, knowing the right reference points is another. The area that we most often paddle (Nanaimo to Duncan) does not have marine reference points in the forecasts. The closest points are Ballenas Islands (to the north), Entrance Island, Strait of Georgia (to the east) and Saturna Island (to the south). These areas are almost always windier than the sheltered area inside the northern Gulf Islands.

Beaufort Scale (0 - 5)

Force	Strength	Wind Speed Km	Wind Speed Knots	Effect
0	calm	0 - 1	0	Smoke rises vertically; sea is calm
1	light air	1 - 5	1 - 3	Smoke drifts; light ripples
2	slight breeze	6 - 11	4 - 6	Leaves rustle, weather vanes move, wind felt on face; small wavelets
3	gentle breeze	12 - 19	7 - 10	Light flags unfurl, leaves and twigs on trees move steadily; long unbreaking waves
4	moderate breeze	20 - 28	11 - 16	Small branches move, loose dust and paper fly about; waves with whitecaps
5	fresh breeze	29 - 38	17 - 21	moderate waves with many whitecaps

Weather reports often speak about 'highs' and 'lows'. This difference is called a pressure gradient, which is the net difference between a high and low. Winds travel from a high to a low and are affected by the earth as it spins (Coriolis force). This force deflects the winds to the right in the Northern Hemisphere. There are many factors from centrifugal force to friction that influence how winds travel.

When you're planning a paddle, familiarity with local sea and land breezes will be helpful. It is quite possible the area where you will kayak will be protected from mainstream winds but locally produced breezes can be a factor.

Sea breezes occur as the result of bodies of land and water heating up and cooling down at different rates. Sea breezes most often happen on warm sunny days during the spring and summer when the temperature of the land is typically higher than the temperature of the ocean. In the morning the land and the water start out at similar temperatures. As the sun beats down on the land and sea the land heats quickly while the sea or ocean stays at a more constant temperature because it can absorb a lot of heat without warming. Once a significant differential of temperature exists, the sea breeze begins blowing onto shore.

Land breezes are common in the fall and winter and begin with the cooling of low air. On a calm evening, a differential of temperature between nearby land and water occur causing a cool wind to blow offshore. This wind is called a "land breeze". A land breeze is stronger closer to the coastline.

We have often gone paddling when the marine forecast has predicted a 'small craft warning'. While, we do not advise paddlers to take chances, generally, we use our knowledge of the many places to kayak and choose a more protected spot. Usually if strong winds are predicted or weather conditions look unstable then we eliminate open crossings from our paddling route. We also look at wind direction and eliminate areas with large open bodies of water in those directions where waves could build in height. We have paddled many times in wind that will blow the hat off your head, but there was not a large expanse of water on the windward side of us, so the waves were tiny.

Some of the more sheltered local areas are Ladysmith Harbour (which is almost always a safe and ideal paddling location), Nanaimo Harbour, the inside portions of Piper's Lagoon and Hammond Bay, and often the area from Cedar-by-the-Sea boat launch to Blue Heron Park in Yellow Point. Some of the most windy areas we have encountered locally include the northern Nanaimo area (Neck Point, and the outside portion of Piper's Lagoon), Sansum Narrows and Maple Bay. We have often found the Chemainus area and Cowichan Bay to be windy if the wind is from the southeast. Several times we have taken a choppy ferry ride over to Gabriola Island to paddle among the Flat Top Islands and found it flat calm after a drive across to the other side of the island.

As most of the local paddling is at least partially sheltered, there is usually somewhere you can paddle locally without exceeding your comfort level. An added benefit to being a kayaker is that you become much more attune to winds, weather, tides and currents.

A long ways from home - Gary kayaking on the Yukon River

Filing a float plan

You should always file a float plan whether you're heading off for a day paddle or for an extended trip. The float plan might be as simple as letting someone know where you're launching, who you're paddling with, your proposed route and when you plan to return. The idea is to let that person know when to call out a search party and where that party should search. Hopefully you will never be the subject of a search party, but it pays to be safe.

A sample Float Plan form is shown on the following page.

Float Plan
Let family or friends
know where you are

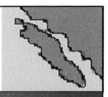

Route Information

Launch Site:
Proposed Route: (describe)

Planned Date and Time of Return:

Paddler Information

Name: Type of Boats:
Phone #: (   )   Distinguishing Colours:
Cell #:   # of Paddlers:
E-mail: # of Boats:
VHF Radio: (Yes) (No)

> Shore contact person:
> Phone #: (   )
> Remember to notify this person upon your
> return!!!

Vehicular Information

Vehicle License:
Type of Vehicle:
Colour:
Located at:

Equipment Checklist

Charts	First aid kit	Tide table	Compass
Rain gear	Tent	Pump	Paddle float
Repair kit	Spray skirt	Matches	VHF radio
GPS	Spare paddle	Food	Water bottle
Water supply	Clothing	Sunglasses	Hat
Sleeping bag	PFD	Personal items	Knife
Toilet paper	Book	Utensils	Rope
Seat cushion	Snacks	Paddle	

Other

Rescue Coordination Center: 1 (800) 567-5111
Information: www.easykayaker.com
Weather: www.weatheroffice.com

Section 3—Buying a Kayak

Buying sea kayaks

When it comes time to buy your first kayak, if you haven't done much paddling, it can be a difficult decision-making process. They say good judgment comes from experience *and a lot of that comes from bad judgment.* Reading about kayak design and talking to experienced kayakers will help. Talking to *really* experienced kayakers (fanatic kayakers) may just confuse you, as boat design and performance is a never-ending nonstop topic with these guys.

Before someone can give you much guidance in choosing a kayak, there are a few decisions you'll have to make. Do you want to buy a double or single kayak? Doubles are very stable, but not nearly as much fun to paddle as a single. Next decision, what type of paddling are you planning to do, mostly day trips, overnighters, or do you want to be able to head off on weeklong journeys? Lastly, what kind of paddler do you want to be, fair weather or all-weather?

Once you've decided the double vs. single question, people most often go for a compromise in regards to the rest. They look for a boat that is great for day paddles and yet suitable for tripping. Usually stability wins out over speed so that paddling the boat will be within your comfort zone in most normal weather conditions.

Generally, the longer and more narrow the kayak, the faster it is. The term "speed" or calling a boat "fast" seems out of place when talking about easykayaking. Although a fast boat is obviously faster than a slow boat, that's not what I'm really talking about. A fast boat slides through the water gracefully with little effort, a real joy to paddle. The distance that a person can cover increases and new paddling areas become accessible with a "faster" boat, plus it's easier to keep up with the group.

Stability on the other hand is paramount to safety. Slipping through the water with ease is only great if you can do it right side up. Most popular ocean touring single kayaks are around 24" to 25" wide. Although this is the width we started with, my daughter and I have now advanced to paddling 22" wide kayaks. The chine (transition between sides and bottom) and the shape of the bottom contribute a lot toward stability. Normally a soft chine (rounded transition) and a flat but somewhat rounded bottom give the best stability.

There are two aspects of stability to be aware of. Initial stability is how tippy a kayak feels when you are sitting still in calm water. If the boat shifts every time you move slightly, photography, fishing and other activities can be difficult, plus it's hard to relax. Secondary stability is the tip over type of stability. Most rental outfits and adventure tour guides buy kayaks that have both good initial and secondary stability. Some kayaks have one but not the other.

Hull shapes may be symmetrical, fish form or swedeform. Hull shapes and rocker (upturn of hull when viewed from the side) affect tracking and turning as well as speed and stability. There is also flare to consider (shape of the sides) and whether you should have a swept up bow or more of a straight nose to your boat. A swept up bow catches the wind, but may surf better and many kayakers think it looks better too. Does the boat have a rudder or skeg (fixed or retractable fin like rudder for tracking straight) and will you need one?

Confused yet? If you aren't an expert in kayak design (and even the experts don't agree among themselves), then it's time to rely on some basic principles. Does the boat feel good when you paddle it normally and how does it feel when you try a short power paddle at full speed? This power paddle is a good indication of how the boat will handle under rougher weather conditions plus how well it slips through the water. Is this a model that outfitters buy? Do you like the look of the kayak and does it fit you well?

Now for the question of buying new or used. Paul will guide you through buying a used kayak and I'll help with information on buying a new kayak. We have each included information that is applicable to the other's topic so it will be worthwhile to read both sections whether you're buying new or used.

Buying a used sea kayak

When I bought my first boat I hadn't read about design characteristics, strength, handling, models or anything else. I just knew I wanted a boat that was seaworthy. To me this meant a boat that wouldn't tip in adverse conditions and would keep me safe!

I've bought three used kayaks: a single plastic (polyethylene roto-molded) model, a single fibreglass model, and a plastic double. I've found that a fibreglass hull is faster, lighter, and simply more attractive. Plastic kayaks cost less money and are much stronger. Fibreglass boats appear to last quite a bit longer when subjected to ultraviolet light than plastic or wood. Wood kayaks are often beautiful and masterful pieces of art and a very personal decision to either buy or build. If you are to the point of building a wooden craft, you have likely studied design, handling, and other characteristics, and have made a personal choice for wood. All in all, I favour fibreglass kayaks for a number of reasons including durability, weight, design, and resale.

Before you buy a sea kayak you need to understand some fundamental principles of their design. There are many types of kayaks on the market and most do a good job in various weather conditions. The most fundamental trade-off in boat design is tracking versus turning. A kayak that tracks well or goes straight typically does not turn as quickly. In contrast, a kayak that turns well does not track well. If you're going on long journeys where turning is not as important, the tracking ability of the kayak will be more important to you.

You want to have enough knowledge of your purchase to feel good about it so we recommend that you try out the secondhand kayak for stability. Outfitters often comment on how certain manufactured kayaks are more stable than others. They want their first-time customers to feel safe. Initial stability of a kayak is the ease in which a kayak will begin to tip. If you like to troll from your boat or photograph the local wildlife choose a boat with initial stability. Secondary stability is the force it takes to tip a kayak over.

Kayak manufacturers usually produce a full line of kayaks for every imaginable type of paddler. Kayakers and kayaks both come in all shapes and sizes. The width and shape of the hull along with length and general design all factor into the stability. Beginners often buy a kayak with better initial stability and an advanced paddler will consider different features.

I must admit the most important characteristic for me in a sea kayak is comfort. I like a sea kayak that pads my back really well. I hate aching for the last half of my paddle-day. You can add padding for your butt, knees, and back. A really fast kayak has little meaning to me unless I am completely comfortable.

Once you have found the used kayak to be stable and comfortable you can now examine other features. Are the hatch covers easy to take off? Are the hatch covers waterproof? What type of rudder system is on the boat? Does the rudder lift and re-sit easily? Is the rudder a sliding foot-operated system or a tilt pedal system? You may have to ask an experienced kayaker about some of these features, or search the Internet for specifics.

When is the best time to buy a used kayak? Generally, the early fall or late summer is best. Many outfitters sell their complete stock when their season is over. When I bought my fibreglass boat I went to several outfitters. Many of the scratches and scuff marks can be buffed out but I based my decision on the general appearance of the boat and looked for any serious gouges. Some outfitters are more fussy than others in regard to how their clients treat their kayaks while others don't seem to care as much. Like many kayakers I do plan to sell my boat again and try to keep it in excellent condition for resale. Buying a kayak from a strictly rental outfit might be dicier than from an outfitter/guide company. More often than not, rentals are dragged up the beach across barnacles and over logs and are generally abused. We have seen many first hand cases of this. Look in local kayak web sites, magazines, and newspapers for private sales.

A used plastic sea kayak sells for between $1000 – $1400 (Cdn). Look for the seller to include a paddle, skirt, paddle float, PFD, and other accessories. If you can buy these used, you should be able to save a fair amount of money. A used fibreglass sea kayak normally sells for $1800 – $2400. Double kayaks are more expensive. Whether to buy a single or double will depend on your situation. Eventually, most kayakers like to own a single. It may require four people to carry a fully loaded double kayak up the beach. Doubles are incredibly stable but are also more difficult to upright and pump out.

Vancouver Island Paddlefest 2000
a great place to try out kayaks

Look at several kayaks, compare them, and try them out. The more stable models tend to be a bit wider (usually around 24" – 25") and are most suitable for the beginner kayaker. Ask (or find out) how it handles in rougher waters.

Ultraviolet (UV) is the biggest factor causing deterioration of both plastic and fibreglass kayaks. If the kayak you're thinking of buying has suffered UV degradation, it will be apparent and easy to spot by looking for colour fade and the breakdown of neoprene hatch covers and deck shock cords. By lifting the hatch covers and comparing the colour of the deck where it was shaded by the hatch cover against the deck colour where it was not shaded, you should be able to see if any fading has taken occurred.

Next, inspect the hull and deck for cracks, gouges and scratches. Gouges and scratches can be repaired easily and are good indicators of how much and hard a kayak has been used, but cracks are more serious.

The tip of the bow and the rudder area should be looked at for signs of hard impacts and wear around moveable parts. Check the rudder blade to see if it's bent and check the bracket that mounts the rudder to the kayak. If the bracket is bent, it is an indication of a mishap with something hard.

Check the seal on bulkheads and hatches and ask if the boat leaks at all. You can fill the hatches partway with water and stand the boat on end to test bulkheads. Some bulkheads have an intentional pinhole to prevent potential pressurization problems.

It isn't easy to determine the use vs. abuse factor of a used kayak. Is the wear and tear an indication of a lot of normal use or an indication of abuse? One way to tell is to look at the area below the rudder pedals (or foot braces) for signs of wear. Just like the floor mat in a car, the paddler's feet wear this area. You should also examine the inside of the front and rear hatches by the bulkheads. This is supposed to be where heavy items are stored when paddling and will show signs of wear if the kayak has been used a lot for camping. Lastly, look at the rope that raises and lowers the rudder. The last few inches at the rudder end will give some indication of how many times that rudder has gone up and down by the amount of wear it shows.

Ask about the kayak's age. Most fibreglass kayaks have a serial number on the hull near the rudder. This serial number will include the date of manufacture. A serial number such as QKN004890998 would indicate that the boat was made in September 1998. If looked after and protected from UV when not in use, a fibreglass kayak should last 30 years. Plastic boats aren't so lucky and will probably have a lifespan of about 10 to 15 years. If exposed to UV when not in use, plastic boats will have a lifespan of only about 7 or 8 years.

Finally, paddle the kayak you like for at least an hour and decide if it's comfortable and sits in the water the way you like. It takes a few paddling trips to get seatbacks, rudder pedals and padding just the way you like them, but on your first test paddle you should be able to get a pretty good feel for the boat.

Buying a new sea kayak

There are many advantages of buying a new kayak as opposed to a used kayak. First, you aren't limited to choosing the makes and models currently for sale on the used market. Next, you can choose the colours and options you want. Also, the boat will be in brand new condition and it will come with a warranty. The disadvantages of buying new over used, include having to pay about $400 to $1000 more than you would for a used kayak and having to wait for your boat to be built (unless you buy off the rack).

I've bought five new kayaks and four used kayaks. My waiting period for the new boats ranged from one to five months. One disadvantage to buying a new kayak is paying PST and GST. There's no tax if you buy a used kayak from an individual, but buying a used kayak from an outfitter normally requires paying PST and GST.

A kayak should fit you, your experience level and the type of paddling

you plan to do. I didn't know much about paddles or PFDs (lifejackets) when I bought my first kayak, but just like kayaks these items should be fitted to you. So how do you find the right boat, paddle and PFD? My first stop is to go surfing. On the web, not with a kayak, although that's fun too. The Easykayaker website has links to all the main Pacific Northwest kayak manufacturers' websites. If you click in the right place on their website and provide them with your mailing address, most manufacturers will send you a brochure and list of dealers.

Most manufacturers' catalogs include good descriptions of their kayaks in relation to the type of person and paddling each boat is designed for along with handling characteristics of each kayak. Also included are specifications for weight, length, width, depth and volume. Volume tells you two things. First, it's a good indication of how much gear you can pack in for tripping, but secondly how much weight the boat will support. Many larger kayak models come in either standard or high volume models. Usually the difference between a standard and high volume kayak of the same model is that the high volume model is about ¾" greater in depth. An added advantage of a high volume boat is that the extra depth makes the boat easier to get in and out of. The higher volume boats can present some disadvantages for smaller paddlers.

Once you decide on a boat or at least narrow the choices down, test paddling is a must. Many dealers and manufacturers have demo boats or agreements with rental outfits to facilitate this.

Some manufacturers offer a wide variety of colours to choose from. Seaward is one of the leaders in this area. You can choose the hull colour, the deck colour, the hatch colour, the coaming colour and the edge strip (seam) colour. Their 1999 catalog stated that that there are 614,655 possible variations with the 28 stock colours. If that's not enough, they do custom colours, fades and custom artwork. I saw one boat finished to look like a Dolly-Varden trout. As much as I like the looks of the fades, metallics and splatters, these are very difficult to touch up later on. Two final considerations are that darker colours show scratches more (this is why most kayak bottoms are white) and that bright deck colours make your kayak more visible to larger boats and therefore are safer.

Some manufacturers offer a variety of additional options depending on the kayak model. Options may include a compass, choice of seats, thigh braces, an under deck bag (above your knees), a day hatch (for lunch and rain gear) and soft deck fittings. Rudders, rudder controls and skegs may also be options. Also, some manufacturers even offer you a choice of extra reinforcing layups, kevlar layups, and graphite layups.

Kayaks become very personal objects. Buying a custom made kayak especially designed for you with your choice of options can give you a greater sense of pride in what you end up paddling.

Section 4—Kayak Care, Handling, Maintenance and Repair

Care and maintenance for your kayak

This list is very basic. Refer to your dealer/manufacturer or an article on kayak care for further information:

- Salt corrodes metal fittings. After each use give your kayak a wash with fresh water
- Check all screws, nuts and fittings for tightness every few months
- Store your kayak on fitted padded rests. Your kayak can lose its shape if left sitting on a flat or rugged surface. Preferably the rests should be placed close to the bulkheads
- UV destroys plastic and fibreglass. Keep your kayak out of the sun during storage. Protect your kayak by applying an UV protectant coating
- Inspect your kayak for wear and tear. Inspect components that could break. Replace anything that is beginning to wear. Make sure neoprene hatch covers are in good shape. Never paddle a boat without watertight hatch covers unless your boat has tapered buoyancy air bags
- Inspect the spring that locks the paddles together
- Check your foot braces or sliders for wear
- Inspect your rudder or skeg control. Use WD-40 or silicone spray for lubrication
- DO NOT drag your boat on the beach. Do not sit on the hatches or decks when the kayak is out of the water
- When car topping, tie tight across the kayak but allow bow and stern tie-downs to be slightly loose. Do not let the boat fill with rain and then drive over rough terrain. Be very careful that the bowline doesn't become untied and is driven over (unless you want a broken boat). Use straps or ropes, not bungy cords, to tie your boat to your car rack
- Fully loaded kayaks should not be carried by only the handles, but should also be supported by a hand under the keel as too much

stress on the carrying handles could cause damage to the kayak
- Fibreglass kayaks should be treated with a boat cleaning/polishing/ wax compound at least once a year. Not only will your kayak look better, it will also glide through the water much easier

Kayak repair

Kayaks are made from wood, cloth, plastic, fibreglass and other materials. It would take an entire book to discuss all the different kayak repairs that might be needed. The following is a brief guide to repairing some of the more common problems.

Replacements for worn or damaged fittings and components such as rudders, seats, hatch covers, bungies, handles, etc. can be bought from most dealers. For those who don't want to do their own repairs or if the damage is more serious, manufacturers and dealers often offer repair services.

Scratches on plastic boats can be removed with heat using a blowtorch with a wide tip or an electric iron. Only an experienced person should do this. If you think you might want to try it yourself, practice on a plastic five-gallon bucket first. Damaged hulls can be heat welded by an expert although I've heard of one occasion where this was done using a campfire and a plastic bucket found on the beach in an emergency situation in order to get home.

Fibreglass kayaks are very repairable. Before attempting any fibreglass repairs however, visit your bookstore or library and read up on working with fibreglass. Fortunately, fibreglass is quite easy to work with and requires few tools. Small cans of coloured gel-coat to match your boat can be bought from the kayak manufacturer. These are good for fixing gouges and deep

Who put that rock there?

scratches. Fibreglass cloth can be added to areas worn thin or damaged.

For faded fibreglass boats, a good cut polishing often brings the colour back. Make sure you treat the boat with an UV protective coating after cut polishing. For boats that need more than just polishing, they can be successfully painted with fibreglass paint. For best results, have the painting done by an auto body shop.

Kayaker etiquette

A friend once said, "If you're not polluting and making noise, you're not having fun!" He was joking, but for some 'boaters' that's not far from the truth. Fortunately, most kayakers are a totally different breed of boaters. On the whole, we are a caring group of people that enjoy nature and respect the environment. Nonetheless, we all need reminders sometimes, so here are a few gentle hints of etiquette.

Ideally your paddling should not alter the behavior of wildlife. It's okay to observe, but give the marine mammals a little space. When landing on a beach, if you scare sea birds off their nests, their young or eggs can quickly be gobbled up by the competition.

- Respect private property rights above high tide and shellfish lease areas below high tide
- If you are paddling with people less experienced, assume the role as leader in as far as looking out for your group's safety and comfort. This also includes helping others on the beach launching and landing
- Rules of the road are that the kayak in front of you has the right-of-way. Do not bump into their kayak. Rudders are easily damaged if struck by a following kayak
- Do not step over another person's kayak (especially my kayak)
- Do not move someone's kayak without asking them first. This rule can be broken if the tide is about to float it away or some other danger is eminent
- Use your whistle sparingly. It is for safety. Have a group code. Usually one long blast means all stop and help, two short blasts of the whistle means all stop
- Lastly, practice low-impact environmental paddling. This includes leaving nothing behind, not even banana or orange peels

Section 5—Kayak Camping

Kayak camping

Compared to backpacking, kayak camping is outdoor luxury. Now, there are those people whose idea of luxury camping is to drive the motorhome to a crowded public campground. But for those of us who are into wilderness camping away from the madding crowd, the kayak affords this to be done in style, complete with table cloth and stemware if that is your desire.

Unless you plan to portage your kayak some distance, weight is not too much of a concern when preparing your camping list. Volume and durability should be a factor though. For example, I would choose bagels over a loaf of bread as bagels take up less room and don't get squished as easily when packed tightly in a hatch. Bread will also become stale and/or moldy long before bagels will.

Most single sea kayaks will hold an incredible volume of camping gear. Some doubles can carry a phenomenal load. Paul and I can completely fill the back of my 4Runner (with the seats folded down) and somehow get everything but the coolers into the two boats. It was an awesome sight to see how much eight of us loaded into the boats for our Gulf Island tour two years ago. Actually, it was disgusting that we took so much for five days, but we weren't lacking for anything and it did all fit.

Ideally you should look after life's necessities such as food, clothing and shelter, after that you add niceties like toilet paper and finally luxuries.

I strongly recommend that you create a camping list of everything you might want to take and use the list as a checklist for future trips. You will probably modify it a half dozen times, but eventually you will have a perfect quick packing list for your needs and wants. The reason I suggest a broad form list instead of a concise list is that your packing will vary depending on the season, the location and the length of each trip. It may also vary because of who you are paddling with, especially if you are sharing gear (like cooking equipment) and are sharing meals.

Pre-trip

These are the things that I do a day or two before the trip.
- get tide tables & chart for the area we will be paddling
- get or find fishing license if needed
- check Coleman stove and make sure it's full and still works
- buy Coleman stove fuel (if needed) and fill bottles
- buy food for the trip
- contact whoever will be looking after our livestock and pets
- buy or locate a good book for leisure reading
- buy any items that I'm missing from the list below
- make a thick crust sourdough bread for day number one of the trip
- pre-mix bannock and dumpling dry ingredients

Camping list

A list of things to possibly take
- tent that isn't larger than you really need to be comfortable
- one or two small tarps (I use one as a blanket to put my gear on when packing or unpacking my kayak. Later it gets used as a doormat for my tent and if it rains hard and long the tarps get used for protection from the rain).
- air mattresses or ground pad for under the sleeping bag (I have tried foam pads, self inflating units, but still prefer an air mattress for a good night's sleep)
- small air pump (if using an air mattress)
- clothes
- long underwear (just in case)
- coats (usually polar fleece or Gortex)
- swim suit or quick dry shorts for swimming
- rain gear (paddling jacket will often do for a top and rain pants for the other half)
- sandals and hiking shoes
- hats (for shade, for rain and a toque for warmth)
- light rope or cord (for hanging food in trees, for a clothesline and many other uses)

- sunglasses
- sunscreen
- sleeping bag
- fishing gear
- bait
- crab trap
- cell phone
- towels
- dish rag/scouring pad
- dish (sea) soap
- toothbrush/paste/floss
- Q tips
- toilet paper
- glasses
- books
- flashlight/radio
- matches/firestarter
- money
- hair stuff
- camp shovel
- basic medicines
- garbage bags
- backpacks
- first aid box
- nails & axe
- silverware
- plates
- bowls
- cups & stemware
- pots
- frying pan
- coffee pot
- paring knife
- peeler
- pancake flipper
- can opener
- Coleman stove
- Coleman fuel
- pocket knife
- Leatherman

- compass
- daypack
- lip balm
- camera/film
- insect repellent
- ziplock bags
- water bottles
- hammock
- candle lantern
- foxtail ball
- kite and string
- needle and thread
- safety pins
- tinfoil
- Tupperware
- water
- water purifier
- marine chart
- tidetable
- camp area map
- camp chairs
- sheet
- duct tape

Kayak gear:
- PFD (lifejacket)
- sprayskirt
- paddlefloat
- seat pad
- paddle & spare
- kayak
- water bottle
- GPS / compass
- weather radio
- sponge
- tow rope
- paddling boots/gloves

Clothing

If one could be sure of the coastal weather, choosing which clothes to pack for a summer kayak camping trip would be simple. Quick dry shorts and tops or t-shirts for paddling. Add a pair of long pants and a long sleeved shirt for evenings and early mornings. Include polar fleece and long underwear in case the weather turns cold at night. A few favourite camping clothes are great to bring along. I have a shirt with animal tracks on it and we often use it to identify the prints in the sand. My daughter has a camping favourite passed down from her cousins Calista and Anthony, which is a shirt that has printed on it "Same shirt—different day".

We usually take one pair of walking shoes for evenings and light hiking. During the day when not paddling we wear sandals or go barefoot. We each include a baseball style cap and knit toque for headwear plus a rain hat or sou'west'r for protection from rain. Raingear is a must for Vancouver Island because clothes won't dry if you get them wet when the weather is cool.

Humidity levels are typically high while paddling and when on the beach. Undershirts that wick moisture away from your skin such as silk and some of the synthetics are desirable. Synthetic long underwear will keep you warmer at night than cotton fabrics. For those who can handle it next to their skin, wool is also an excellent fabric for warmth in a moist environment.

Meal planning

Diet is really a personal thing, but there are a few things you may want to consider. First and foremost, how much time do you want to spend preparing meals? On leisurely trips, meal prep and eating may be a main social event. On the other hand, if the 'chief cook and bottle washer' part of you decides that he/she wants a holiday, you may want to opt for quick easy meals like bagels and cream cheese, a handful of nuts, something to drink, and a cookie or chocolate for dessert.

Usually a combination of a few gourmet meals and some basic easy meals works best. Having some no-cook foods for lunches and breakfasts is wise. If you are unfortunate enough to hit a patch of rainy weather these no-cook meals will come in handy. We always take extra food and water in case we end up staying an extra couple of days. This extra food also gives us an option to cook or not to cook, depending on our mood at the time.

Our group has developed a nice routine, such that we each look after our own breakfasts and lunches (though we usually do share), and we take turns preparing communal suppers for the whole group. This works well for a group of five or less, but cooking for six or more is not as easy with small pots and one burner stoves.

I buy all my food at the grocery store. I don't spend the extra money for freeze-dried backpacking/camping foods. As mentioned previously, foods can be heavy but I try to avoid bulky items. Bagels travel well. Canned food such as stew makes for easy meals. Fruits and fresh veggies are always a treat. Trail mix and cookies are standard operating procedure. An important aspect is that each kayaker has a different trail mix. I like the mix with dried fruit and Smarties mixed in. And don't let me catch someone picking out all the Smarties.

Sharing food with fellow campers is nice, but mice, squirrels, crows, raccoons and depending on location, bears, would all like to share your food too. You won't have to worry about bears in the Gulf Islands or the Broken Group, but for safety I never bring food into my tent, as I sometimes use the same tent in bear country. We either store food in the kayak hatches or hang it from trees overnight. We use bird and squirrel proof containers inside net bags to hang our food in the trees. Most mornings I find raccoon prints on my kayak. I'm glad they haven't learned how to open hatches yet. One night we left a tall dirty hot chocolate mug on a log for washing the next morning only to find we had caught a live mouse in it.

Sample food lists

Breakfasts (4)
ziplock bags (for cooking omelets)
eggs
cream cheese
green onions
cheddar cheese
fruit
pancake mix
syrup
margarine
jam
hot or cold cereal
instant milk

Lunches (3)
sour dough bread
bagels
cream cheese
cheese
jam
margarine
fig newtons
pop
pepperoni/salami
bannock
trail mix
fruit

Dinners:

(Note: By the time you are ready to cook dinner on the first night, you are usually a wee bit tired from last minute packing, driving to the launch site, packing your kayaks, paddling to your destination and setting up camp. Dinner #1 should be simple and easy. We will often freeze a precooked meal and heat & serve it the first night.)

Dinner 1
Pre-cooked Himalayan Stir-fry
Frozen or refrigerated pre-cooked meal (heat and serve)

Dinner 2
Stew, Dumplings & Caesar Salad
frozen or canned stew
dry dumplings premixed
Romaine lettuce
Et Tu Caesar mix

Dinner 3
Tacos
tortillas
cheese
refried beans
lettuce/sprouts
tomatoes
sour cream
salsa
canned meat
onions
green peppers

Dinner 4
Greek salad & pasta
feta cheese
tomatoes
cucumbers
olives
red onion
green peppers
oregano
olive oil
pasta mix
margarine

Snacks
cereal bars
cookies
apple/rhubarb sauce
trail mix

Appy
crackers
pickles
cream cheese
cheese
smoked oysters

Dessert
carrot cake, pound cake
candy bars

Drinks
hot chocolate, juice
pop, alcohol

Loading your kayak

Like diet, how you load your kayak is a personal thing. For safety, keep heavy objects low and away from the bow or stern and minimize the amount of objects on deck. Ideally you want to keep the centre of gravity as low as possible and close to the cockpit. Objects on deck under the bungy cords can catch the wind, interfere with wet-entries and be lost easily. I usually keep a spare paddle, paddle float, water bottle and a chart on deck. I sometimes will have a converted fanny pack with lip balm, snacks, etc. in it on deck if the conditions are mild.

My preference for loading is to put tent, sleeping bag and clothes in the rear hatch. Food and cooking supplies go in the front hatch. I have a small daypack of "possibles" that goes last in the front hatch. This contains anything I might want during the day, such as lunch, Swiss army knife, weather radio, GPS, duct tape and first aid kit. Next to this pack is my raingear so it will be quickly accessible.

Behind my seat in the cockpit area is a sponge, water pump, water bottles (I often use two-litre pop bottles), my camp shoes and my paddling jacket (unless I'm wearing it). My shoes are kept high enough in the pile to stay dry and my jacket is positioned that I can reach it while paddling.

I also tend to pick up one or two treasures along the way and these also go behind the seat. These treasures come home and go on a special shelf, which is my sanity shelf. They are my link to paddling when I'm not kayaking. Many of these treasures have the date and trip location written on the back. Near the end of the trip, we usually have a bag or two of garbage and this sometimes goes behind the seat where the water had been (the two-litre pop bottles get flattened).

I have retrofitted the inside of my kayak's cockpit with an above-the-knees net shelf. This net device holds my camera, binoculars and ziplock bag of toilet paper and matches.

The last thing I load in the rear hatch is my small 6'x8' tarp. When packing and unpacking, this tarp is spread out on the beach against the kayak. I usually spread out all of my gear on the tarp before proceeding with the advanced engineering feat of utilizing my cargo space to the nth degree. Things that I'm less likely to need are usually loaded in the narrow and hard to reach pointy ends at bow and stern. Items unfortunately tend to become stuck in these areas and we are now starting to tie strings to them. It also helps to have the bow downhill when loading the forward hatch and uphill when unloading it.

My PFD has pockets, so I carry my tidetable, sunglasses, gloves, spare compass and flares in these pockets. Most PFDs don't have this many pockets, but paddling jackets often have pocket space.

Camping etiquette

Ten years ago if you were a sea kayaker, most likely you were also a true outdoors person with a lot of wilderness savvy. Kayaking as a sport is growing at a tremendous rate, about 20% per year in British Columbia. Many of these new kayakers are also new to wilderness camping.

Conflicts are becoming more frequent between kayakers and landowners, First Nations, power boaters and other kayakers. Most of these conflicts stem from a lack of awareness. Unfortunately, as a result of these conflicts, private lands traditionally used by kayakers are now becoming closed to camping and the overall reputation of kayakers in general has suffered. With this in mind, we offer the following general guidelines about protocol and etiquette concerning kayaking and wilderness travel.

Let's start with the beginning of your trip. Many kayakers use boat ramps as launch sites. Many boat ramps were built with funds raised by and labour donated by power boaters. Be sensitive to the needs of power boaters when competing for the use of a ramp.

Next, consider how your travel will impact marine wildlife. Ideally your paddling should not alter the behaviour of wildlife. It's okay to observe, but give the marine mammals a reasonable space. If you scare sea birds off their nests when landing on or passing near a beach, their young or eggs can quickly be gobbled up by the competition.

Now let's look at where to camp. Due to the recent popularity of kayaking, the number of kayak campers has grown much faster than the number of campsites and the impact of campers is no longer minimal in many areas. Camping should be in designated campsites when possible. This confines the impact to specific areas. Camping below the high tide line is also an option if the tides cooperate. Try to camp away from water sources and trails to avoid impacting wildlife. Respect private property and cultural sites, and leave artifacts alone!

Minimize the urge to tame the jungle. Campsites should be found, not made. British Columbia's unique flora and fauna can be very fragile. Stick to traveling existing trails and set your tent up in established sites.

Use fire sparingly, but better yet, not at all. In most areas there are no quick ways of putting out a fire that gets away. Even if your fire is well-confined, the potential risk that it causes may be enough to upset other people that visit the area.

Leave no trace that you have been there, especially when camping outside designated campsites. Pack everything out including peelings and food scraps. If you packed it in, then you should pack it out. But why stop there? Why not pick up the litter someone else left to help make up for your impact? There can be a sense of pride knowing you left an area cleaner than you found it.

This may be sounding like a lecture but hopefully your head is nodding in agreement to these principles. So here comes the touchy part, human waste and toilet paper. Everywhere Paul and I have camped in the last four years, we found that people had left this for others to find. Besides the unsightliness and health risk, it attracts animals and diminishes the reputation of kayakers. So what's the alternative? The easiest solution is to camp where an outhouse is available. Other solutions include using a honey bucket or as a last resort digging and using a cat hole. Cat holes should be at least 300 feet away from water sources and not near camping areas or beaches used for swimming.

Washing dishes without impact means disposing of gray water properly and either using no soap or small amounts of low impact soap. Even biodegradable soap will affect intertidal life forms, so use sand for dishwashing and when you do use soap, try to dispose of your gray water far from fresh water and intertidal life.

As kayak camping popularity grows, you may find yourself sharing your campsite with others. Even if you were there first, the campsite is not really "yours." Some people are night owls and others are early risers. Campers should minimize noise between 10:00 P.M. and 8:00 A.M. Loud radios and pets should be left at home. Don't step over another person's kayak and don't move someone's kayak without asking them first unless you see it starting to float away.

A few people camping on a beach each year have little impact. Hundreds and even thousands of people are now camping on many of the best spots available to kayakers around Vancouver Island and the impact is becoming significant. Sea kayaking is a fantastic sport and 99% of the people who take it up are

Blackberry Point - Valdes Island

wonderful caring folks. This article was not intended to criticize anyone, only to help make common sense, common to all kayakers.

The book *Kayak Routes of the Pacific NorthWest Coast*, edited by Peter McGee, is an excellent source for more extensive information on minimal impact camping (ISBN 1-55054-615-5).

Local kayak campsites

The area bounded by Nanaimo, Duncan and the Gulf Islands offers several choice campsites for kayakers. As a special breed of people, who travel under their own power, kayakers usually enjoy nature to a high degree. With that in mind, most kayakers want a campsite that has few non-kayakers watering down the ambiance of the experience. This rules out campsites with road access and to some degree campsites with good moorage. Fortunately many of the marine parks that have good moorage also have spots with poor moorage but good kayak landings.

There are three favourite Easykayaker campsites in the northern Gulf Islands, two of which are British Columbia Provincial Marine Parks and the third is Weyerhaeuser forestry land that has been leased to the BC Marine Trail Association. Pirates Cove Marine Park on DeCourcy Island and Wallace Island Marine Park are the two Provincial Parks sites. The marine trail campsite is Blackberry Point on Valdes Island. BC Parks' website has information available for many of their parks on the web at www.env.gov.bc.ca/bcparks/explore/explore.htm

* * * * *

Pirates Cove Marine Park is a boaters' paradise and the cove side fills up quickly with large boats in the summer. Fortunately the camping and most of the park is facing Ruxton Island on the other side away from the cove and has a great beach for kayakers and swimming. DeCourcy Island is mostly privately owned, but the park is situated such that you don't see the other properties.

There are four well-maintained outhouses and a hand pump for fresh water. Campsites are marked and many have picnic tables. Fires are not allowed. Expect to have deer and raccoons in your campsite at night and if you sleep under the stars you may even get stepped on. Most of the park is a headland connected to DeCourcy by a neck of land and there are great view spots and nice trails on the headland. The narrow dirt roads that loop through the rest of the island are also pleasant for hiking.

Camping at DeCourcy's Pirates Cove Marine Park comes with a fee and they require cash, so bring money. There are 12 walk-in "official" campsites, but of the many visits we have made, seldom have more than half the sites been taken. We camped there a few days before the Labour Day long weekend (see section of Kayaking with Kids) and were the only campers there.

Cedar-by-the-Sea (see section on this launch site) is the launch site

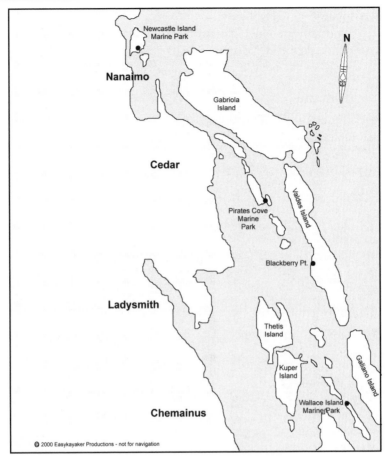

Local Campsites

most often used by paddlers for reaching Pirates Cove, but most of the launch sites between Nanaimo and Chemainus are within a day's paddling. Cedar-by-the-Sea is one of the closest to DeCourcy and the open crossing is fairly short and favourable. For more information visit the BC Parks website for Pirates Cove: http://www.env.gov.bc.ca/bcparks/explore/parkpgs/pirates.htm.

For those interested in local history, Cedar-by-the-Sea, DeCourcy Island and Valdes Island were home to Brother XII's utopian society in the 1920s. There have been several books written about this charismatic man and his followers, much of which is still steeped in mystery. Rumours still persist of buried treasure left behind when he was forced to flee. One of the more recent books is *Brother XII: The Devil of DeCourcy Island*, by Ron MacIsaac.

Wallace Island is a short paddle north from Saltspring Island. In some ways it's a divided island. The kayakers mainly take to the north end at Chivers Point and the motor and sailboats go to Conover Cove on the south end. It takes about an hour to walk the length of the Island on an overgrown old road, which is now a nice trail. The island has great hiking and nice viewscapes. If you want to read more about Wallace Island, David Conover wrote two books about what it was like to live there during his twenty or so years on the island. They are titled *One Man's Island* and *Once Upon an Island*. There are still two privately owned properties on the island, but 90% of the island is a Provincial Marine Park. Chivers Point has several rocky fingers that form a small bay (except at low tide). There are around 8 to 12 developed campsites, but the area can accommodate many more people. I have seen this site totally deserted during prime summer paddling weather and one night when we camped there, I counted 26 kayaks on the shore.

Chivers Point

At low tide there are local reefs teaming with life to explore. There are the standard regulation BC Parks pit-type outhouses and a well with a hand pump near Conover Cove. Water from the well should be boiled before drinking. No fires are allowed on the island. There is a camping fee and during late Spring to early Fall, a park host will visit to collect the fee.

Like DeCourcy Island, deer and raccoons roam the island. There are also some pretty smart crows. Food left unattended may very well go missing. High tide at Chivers Point leaves little room for kayaks on the beach, so choose carefully where you leave your boat. For more information visit the BC Parks website for Wallace Island: www.env.gov.bc.ca/bcparks/explore/parkpgs/wallace.htm.

Southey Point on the northern tip of Saltspring Island is the closest launch site for getting to Wallace Island. Crofton, Chemainus, Thetis Island, Evening Cove or Blue Heron Park are all within a day's paddling to Wallace Island for those who want a longer kayak trip.

* * * * *

Blackberry Point on Valdes Island is a kayaker's campsite. This camping area was made possible through the efforts of the BC Marine Trail Association (BCMTA) in 1998. The land is private forestland and much of the area is being actively managed for forestry. The BCMTA have installed a solar powered composting toilet and developed nice camping areas. Fire is a very real danger to the forestry on the island and people are requested not to have camp or cooking fires between April and October.

There are huge camping areas in the meadow and also along the beach. The long sandy beach is wonderful for pulling boats up on, for walking along and for swimming. There are some hiking trails on the flats and some mountain goat type trails with great views. The area could easily accommodate a hundred tents, but the line up at the one outhouse might be a bit long. The day we left a very crowded Wallace Island, we arrived at Blackberry Point to find it totally deserted. I've also seen the reverse situation when Blackberry Point has been busy while Wallace Island was not.

* * * * *

There are other parks and campsites in this general area. **Newcastle Island Provincial Marine Park** in the Nanaimo Harbour is one. This is a fantastic park, but not the wilderness type camping most kayakers desire. There are 18 campsites at this park with toilets, showers, water and food concession. Campsite reservations are accepted and first-come, first-served sites are also available. Group campsites are also available. Contact the District office or visit www.env.gov.bc.ca/bcparks/explore/parkpgs/newcastl.htm for more details on these group sites.

Newcastle offers a lot more than kayaking and it's close to Nanaimo's downtown with a foot passenger ferry service. It would be a good choice for youth groups, family camping and for those that don't want to overly "rough it." Even though it's close to downtown, you still feel like you're in the wilds. The 306 hectares of land are covered with large trees and beautiful meadows. There's a good network of trails and many view spots and beaches.

Newcastle Island has an interesting and rich history. Several coal mines stretch under the water to both Protection and Newcastle Island. A huge air vent still exists inland on the northeast side of the island. The openings of the mines can be found on the north end of the island.

Quarries exist on the Newcastle Island Passage side. The sandstone blocks were used in many famous buildings along the West Coast including the San Francisco Mint, which withstood the great earthquake of 1906. Herring salteries, shipyards, and a rich First Nations history are all part of the discovery of this once luxurious Canadian Pacific Railway recreational park. Bill Merilees has recently written a book titled, *Newcastle Island – A Place of Discovery* on the history of the island (ISBN 1-895811-58-9).

Section 6—Kayaking With Kids

Safety considerations, the right boat, making it fun

Each year we see more families kayaking with kids from three years old and up. Having a young child on your lap in calm waters while paddling along the shore is one thing, but we are seeing them on crossings out in the Broken Group on Vancouver Island's West Coast and other exposed areas where I wouldn't paddle without a sprayskirt, let alone with a small child on my lap.

I certainly agree with getting kids out there kayaking at an early age, but to me safety is paramount. For very young children there are double kayaks that have a centre hatch which is convertible into a kid's seat. Current Designs makes their Libra XT with this feature.

Once a child is old enough to paddle effectively (usually somewhere between six and nine years old), putting them in the front cockpit of a short to medium sized double is great. The person in the rear cockpit should be a moderately strong paddler in case you end up paddling against wind and current.

As to the age for paddling a single kayak out in open water, that depends on the child and the type of paddling conditions that might be encountered. My daughter's first solos at age 10 were on the condition that she stay close to my kayak, my towline was on deck, her PFD fitted well and was water tested with her in it. We practiced wet-exits and wet-entries and kept to sheltered waters. Her first crossings in a single were with a large group and she was sandwiched between my boat and her mother's.

When kids do graduate to paddling their own boat, finding one the right size is important if they are going to do a lot of paddling. Katherine did well in a Necky Narpa, but was dwarfed in a Current Designs Solstice

GT high volume. When she was 12, I bought her a Current Designs ST that fits her well. It's 22¼" wide by 17'7" long. The boat has a smaller cockpit than most kayaks, which allows Katherine to brace properly. It's large enough that if she ever outgrows this kayak, her mother will inherit it. Most kayak manufacturers produce some boats that are designed for smaller paddlers, whether they are kids or smaller adults. It's the people that are 6'10" tall (like a fellow kayaker I recently met) that have a hard time finding the right sized kayak.

From this kid's perspective

By Katherine Backlund (age 12)

Kayaking is cool because you can pack a lunch, put it in the roomy front or back hatch of your boat or your buddy's boat, and paddle off to some small island.

Once you get there

Make sure the boats are securely on shore. Then you can explore, eat lunch, build a dam against the tide, play, feed the birds, build a sandcastle, climb a tree, look at the clouds, and it's just you and the people who came with you. Sometimes we play catch with a foxtail (ball with cloth tail). Another fun thing is to throw a chunk of driftwood in the water and then sit on a log and take turns seeing who can hit it with a pebble.

Then if you time it right, drift back with the tide and enjoy a leisurely paddle. This doesn't always happen, but it's great when it does.

Kayaking is fun, it builds muscles and makes you strong. I go kayaking every once and a while with my dad. My favorite thing to do is go with the wind, the tide, and surf. Surfing is really fun, you go really fast, and you're high up on a wave. I have never flipped during surfing. Probably because I'm so small though.

How to surf

To surf you need a fairly windy day, a single kayak (do not try a double, it doesn't work), a paddle, a rudder (it's hard if you don't use it), and a buddy. OK, go launch, get away from any boating channels, and point your nose the same way the waves are going.

Hint: Don't go out in slop, where the waves are big and going in every direction.

Now paddle fairly hard, making sure that your nose is still facing forward. Try to paddle just a little bit slower than the waves are going. Now you will fly with the wind.

Our DeCourcy camping trip

Just before my first year of high school started (8th grade) I asked my dad if Glynis and her dad could come with us to DeCourcy Island for an overnight trip. At the last minute Paul decided to join us. Me and Glynis still want to call him "Mr. Grey" because he used to be our grade three and four teacher. We launched at Cedar-by-the-Sea, rounded Round Island, then paddled through the Hole-in-the-Wall while singing "There's a Hole in the Ground." We stopped for a snack then continued along the northeast side of DeCourcy.

Katherine at age 12

We reached Pirate's Cove Marine Park and pulled our boats up onto the logs on the beach. We carried our tents and gear up to our camping spot. With great difficulty me and Glynis struggled to put up our green two-person tent. Glynis's dad, Bill, set up his tent in front of us and my dad set up his tent to our left, Paul was set up behind and to the left of us.

We put our life jackets, spray skirts and paddles inside the cockpit and then sealed the cockpit cover on so that the wind wouldn't blow our stuff away. We emptied our hatches and carried our air mattresses, sleeping bags, clothes and the rest of our gear to our tent.

Me and Glynis asked our dads if we could go visit Glynis's relatives because they had a girl named Mika that was about our age. The three of us went exploring along the rocky shoreline. Me and Glynis and Mika got to a place where we couldn't go any further but we tried anyway. I jumped onto a rock that was about a foot above the ocean. The top of the rock was dry. The tide was coming in. I couldn't jump back because I couldn't jump that far and that high. I saw some wakes coming from a big boat. I was wearing the only pants that I had and the only shirt that I had. They started saying "Oh no!"

I thought about if I leaned forward I could reach the rocks with my hands but then I wouldn't be able to right myself and I might slip. There was water between the upper rock and the lower rock and I was on the lower rock. I didn't have my lifejacket on. My friends couldn't come and rescue me because they would be stuck too. Then, when the wakes hit, my pants got soaking wet, half way up to my knees. The wakes rolled in one after the other. I tried to jump onto the sandstone rock above me. It was about two feet away from the rock I stood on. I fell against the sandstone rock and grabbed the rock edge with my hands, my body was at about a 45 degree angle. The wakes were rushing in! At this point I was wet to the knees. I pulled myself up onto the rock so my feet were now dangling into the cold water. The waves rushed in and covered my pants with salty water. I pulled myself up the rest of the way, hooking my legs onto the sandstone rock. The three of us biked home in the sun. My dad wasn't very happy when I told him what had happened, but he probably did things like this when he was twelve.

Back at Pirate's Cove, we put on some bathing suits (Mika lent me one of hers) and went splashing along the sandy shore, exploring the tidal pools in the rocks. Mika, Glynis and I walked down to a tiny dock and noticed some small fish swimming around the dock. Glynis noticed some black and white mussels growing under the gangplank. We crushed the mussels between our fingers and fed the meat to the fish. The fish gobbled them up. After the fish got bored and swam away, we got our bikes and rode to the outhouses where we discovered that the Men's smelled a lot better than the Ladies'—we decided to use the Men's outhouse.

On our way home the next day we traveled down the southwest side of DeCourcy Island. The nice breeze and gentle current were helping us. We met Mika and her dad who were paddling a double kayak and rafted up for a few minutes to visit. Next we were off to Cedar-by-the-Sea, which would be the end of our trip. We were ahead of schedule so my dad suggested we stop on a beach at Round Island and swim and watch the seals.

We decided not to swim, but it was fun watching the seals through the binoculars. We told my dad that we would swim if we could use the air mattresses. He agreed and asked if we wanted to ride the air mattresses all the way back to Cedar-by-the-Sea. We took turns blowing up the mattresses.

We were a little apprehensive at first in the cold deep water, but we had our warm PFDs on. We held on to two ropes that were attached to Paul's kayak while my dad towed our empty kayaks. Then Glynis's dad decided to take Glynis in tow and I was left being towed by Paul. Our legs hung down into the water and we thought of giant whales coming to nibble off our toes. The way we sat the air mattress was sticking up in front of and behind us. The water was up to our waists. It was really fun!

Footnote from Dad (Gary)

Katherine and I started paddling together in a short double kayak when she was nine years old. My wife, Teesh, would drop us off at a launch site and pick us up a couple of hours later about 10 km further along the beach.

Kim, the owner of Wildheart Adventures, recommended the Necky Amaruk to me. It's under twenty feet long and easily handled by one person. Besides our day paddles, Katherine and I went on two kayak camping trips together in this boat.

The first was a guided overnighter to Valdes Island. It rained so hard in the middle of the night that Katherine and I both woke up in our small tent and had to shout in order to hear each other even though we were only a foot apart. Katherine's shout stated: "It's too loud!" referring to the noise from the rain. The next morning was sunny and beautiful, but everyone's tents were mud splattered all the way up to the top.

Our second trip was a four day guided trip to Clayoquot Sound with friends and family, plus four strangers who quickly became friends. Our first day out saw us landing in minor surf on a large sandy beach for lunch on the southwest corner of Vargas Island. The guides and one experienced paddler landed first. A wave caught the paddler as his kayak grounded in the sand and he rolled onto his side in the water. The guides were in place to help the rest of us. During the lunch break on the beach, Katherine had a great time playing at the tide line. Unfortunately she got the sleeves of her only long-sleeved shirt wet. This caused her to be chastised by her mother. A few minutes later we were back in the double kayak, sitting at the tide line and waiting for the next big wave. As soon as it arrived the guides gave our boat a shove and off we went climbing over the first breaker. Like most of the other doubles, we were still descending from the first breaker when we hit the second one. Instead of rising up over the second, we dove through the breaker. It was only slightly higher than the top of Katherine's head. A few seconds later we were clear of the small breakers and as I watched the water drip from Katherine's hair, shoulders and arms, a soaking wet Katherine spit out some saltwater and said, "And Mom was mad I got my sleeves wet!"

The last to launch was one of the guides. He got his boat in shallow water, got in and quickly did up his sprayskirt as a wave came in and floated him. As the next breaker rolled over his deck, the sprayskirt popped loose and he had a lap and boat full of water. Fortunately, the warm summer breeze helped us all dry quickly. We certainly gained an appreciation for dangers of surf landings and launches.

We bought a single kayak when Katherine was ten years old. She took to the single right away but could only paddle a few kilometres at a time before tiring out. By eleven years old, she was up to ten kilometres a day and that summer we did a five-day trip in the gulf islands. The weather on the fifth day wasn't great. We did a five-kilometre crossing in whitecapping conditions cutting across the waves at about a 20 degree angle. Teesh, Katherine and I all were paddling single kayaks. I could hear this "Weeee!-

splash" sound as Katherine rose up over each wave and came splashing down the other side. There were eight of us in all, making the journey and I was quite proud of Katherine that she was able to make the crossing without a rest or need of a tow. Like bicycles, kayaks are more stable when moving and the paddles are in the water.

Speaking of towing, no matter whom I go out paddling with, the tow cord is always near at hand. It is a fifty-foot rope (nylon cord) with a safety hook on each end. I attach one end to the bow of the boat I'm going to tow, play out the rope and then make a loop around the outside of my PFD at chest height. By attaching at my chest level, the cord clears my rudder while towing. If you are going to tow someone, it is wise to hook up the towline before getting into rough water. I ask the person I'm towing to put up their rudder and not to paddle. As long as the person you are towing is directly behind you, your boat should remain stable. (Note: many experts suggest attaching the tow rope to your boat, not around your PFD.)

My wife almost caused me to tip over once when I was towing her. After I had towed her for a while she was feeling rested and unknowing to me, she started paddling. When she got beside me the towline gave me an unexpected sideways yank. This impressed both of us with the importance of keeping the boat being towed behind the boat doing the towing. We were in good sized chop in between Maple Bay and Sansum Narrows at the time.

Adventure to Blackberry Point

by Jordan Grey (age 13)

In August 1999, both our families were up at the crack of dawn packing our last supplies for a ferry trip to Thetis Island where we would launch our kayaks. It was nearly 12 P.M. as our car reached the launch point. The launch site is not that far from the Thetis ferry. We dropped our kayaks down a bank about eight feet high. We would launch between Thetis and Kuper Island in a narrow channel. As it turned out the water was flowing quite fast in the wrong direction so we had to work hard to launch.

We packed our

kayaks and prepared ourselves for a four-day journey. I helped pack a single and a double kayak with my mom and dad. It wasn't long before we were in a wider, open area between the two islands and I could see small silver and white fish scurrying away from the shadow of our kayaks as we paddled along. Soon we left Clam Bay and headed for Norway Island.

I'm 13 years old and haven't done a lot of paddling yet. I found I got tired easily and sometimes bored especially when we had to do long crossings. It always helps if your parents can tow you for a while to give you a breather. My dad ties a rope around his waist and then attaches it to my kayak (if I'm in the single). Make sure you keep your boat lined up right behind your parents because it causes a lot of drag or pull. My dad gets tired after 1 or 2 kilometres of towing.

It was a fairly rough crossing to Norway Island. I was in the double with my mom. She asked me to paddle harder as we headed into the wind. You go much faster too if you can coordinate your paddle strokes with the other person. Once we reached Norway Island we paddled the next hour close to the shoreline. Finally after paddling for several kilometres we pulled

Jordan and Imelda

onto a large sand beach. "Ahhh" I thought to myself in relief. My shoulders and back were aching badly and my legs were filled with cramps. I vaulted out of my kayak and sat down on the beach to stretch and get the aches out.

I'm usually thirsty and hungry when paddling. I like to buy a Powerade drink and then re-use the bottle for water on my kayak. I keep it tucked right under a cord so I can reach it easily. I like the Powerade bottles because they have a ringed indent so the cord snuggly fits across it. Once I'm out of my kayak my first question to mom is, "I'm thirsty and hungry?" She usually looks at me funny-like so I've learned to keep my snack and an extra drink in the front hatch on top of everything. Once I've had my snack/lunch I like to explore.

I snacked and glanced around and saw three bald eagles and a hawk. The scenery was great. As I was eating potato chips and cheese sandwiches I heard a strange, odd sound. I caught a glimpse of Katherine (my friend) staring at something in the long tall grass. I sluggishly put down my cheese sandwich and headed towards her. "Cool!" I said. It looked like a fully intact set of vertebrae. Was it a cow, whale or horse? I wondered. Maybe it was a wayward, full grown Canadian moose, I theorized—just joking, there are no moose on the islands! "We're going," called my mom over the slender grass. I walked back to the kayaks with Katherine as we chatted about the bones. We paddled along the Secretary Islands that protected us from the winds for another three kilometres until we reached a marine park. I rushed out of my kayak and looked around the small beach on Wallace Island. Afterwards, we unpacked our kayaks and pitched our tents. (When camping on Islands pitch your tent in a sheltered place to protect against wind, rain or storms.) For the next two days we camped on the island and paddled around. (Make sure you tie your kayaks up at night. If they are too close to the water the tide can sweep them out.)

When we were there a youth group of about 18 kayakers arrived and suddenly there were more kayaks than logs on the beach. I was eating Campbell's soup from a bowl at our camp's picnic bench. (I recommend that kids ask their parents for some stuff they like on a kayak camping trip. It makes the trip special for you then.) However, I didn't actually think I was eating anything special but a boy about 14 or 15 from the youth group stopped at my table and looked at my soup. "Ohh!" he cried, "that looks so good." I replied, "It's only canned soup." "I know," he replied almost sadly, "but I've been eating only dried stuff." I just smiled and he wandered off.

Two days later we left for Blackberry Point on the Vancouver Island side of Valdes Island. As we left the protection of the Secretary Islands the waves started to grow and the sea became rough. (Kids—if it is your first time in rough waters it is better to take a double kayak. Double kayaks are more stable and easier to handle in rough waters.) I was in a single kayak paddling with all my might. (When in rough seas do not go as fast as normal and cut into the waves at an angle so you won't tip). As we paddled farther and farther out into the open the seas became more tempestuous. After another hour of paddling we neared Valdes Island and soon we arrived 1 or 2 kilometres south of Blackberry Pt. along the island's shores. We were quite tired but we paddled for another half-hour and landed on shore. One by one we pulled the kayaks up to the beach and got out. We hauled the kayaks up farther onto the beach and right on top of logs. We tied them to trees for safety. As soon and we had tied up the kayaks we looked around for a suitable campsite.

I found I had a lot of spare time on my hands. Here's a list of things to take on the trip: a good book, an extra snack or two (your parents don't have to know everything!—at least according to me and not my mom), beach games like a frisbee, kite, foxtail ball or other games. Also take some good hiking boots in case you find a long trail.

Wandering the beaches at Blackberry is fun. We couldn't have a fire that night but all the adults and kids chatted. I woke up the next morning around eight to feel sun warming our tent. I walked out to see most of our group up and getting ready to cook breakfast. I sat down on a log and watched the waves roll over the beach.

We returned to Thetis Island the next day. The crossing was really rough. I was glad I was in the double. My dad is better at a wet-exit and getting back in a kayak. But I think kids have to be ready for a rough experience too. I took one course in kayaking where I learned to wet-exit. If you're going to go on a long trip especially on a crossing far from shore learn the safety tips about kayaking. Practice bracing and work at a smooth paddle stroke. Well, we finally arrived back at our launch site after a long paddle from Valdes to Thetis Island and then into Clam Bay. We all worked as a team unpacking. Katherine and I helped a lot but I could tell we were both pretty tired. I like kayaking especially paddling along a rocky shore or playing on a beach with a friend. Crossings—well, they're okay, but a lot of work.

Footnote from Dad (Paul)

When children are in the 9 – 13 year old age bracket plan your trips to match their energy and interest levels. Try to minimize crossing times and spend lots of time touring along the shoreline or stopping and playing on a beach. Be prepared to tow children in adverse conditions of wind or current. A child will quickly tire even if they're in a double with you. Keep lots of snacks and drinks on hand. On really hot days paddlers are tempted to take their sprayskirts off. This practice is fine but remember to put sunscreen on your children's legs and other exposed skin areas. Happy cruising with your family!

Section 7—With a Little Help From Your Commercial Friends

Adventure outfitters

Adventure outfitters are companies that provide the equipment and trained guides to take you on a kayak trip. It may be a day paddle, a weeklong expedition or anything in between. Adventure outfitters are also called kayak tour companies. The trips are referred to as guided tours. The Easykayaker website lists more than 75 adventure outfitters for the Vancouver Island area. This industry is part of the growing worldwide market for eco-tourism and adventure-tourism.

Joining an outfitter for a trip in Clayoquot Sound

So with more than 75 companies to choose from, how do you decide which company is going to get your business and give you the trip of a lifetime or maybe just a fantastic day out paddling and viewing wildlife?

Fortunately, most Vancouver Island adventure outfitting companies are good so you are bound to have a great time, especially if the weather cooperates. However some companies are outstanding and can make the experience that much more enjoyable. So here are a few tips and questions to ask to help chose the right outfitter for you.

Boats and equipment: What kind of kayaks do they use? Many companies use fibreglass boats, but some use plastic boats, which are more work to paddle. Will the company guarantee you a single (or double if that's your wish)? Doubles are much more stable but they are not the essence of kayaking and take some of the adventure out of the trip. How old are their kayaks and equipment? Most companies will only keep their boats a maximum of two years.

Type of trip: How many hours will you be paddling in a day and how wild and wooly might the seas be? Some trips are more laid-back and others are quite energetic. Water conditions vary from wide-open Pacific Ocean to protected waterways. How crowded will the campsite(s) be? Many outfitters now have privately leased camping areas to guarantee that you will not have an overcrowded wilderness experience. How primitive will the toilet facilities be? A number of locations will have no facilities, some will have pit type outhouses and some composting toilets—it's all part of the wilderness experience.

Type of clientele: Some outfitters cater to niche markets and this can be a real bonus. If you are a senior or planning to kayak with kids, make sure you find a company that enjoys working with and markets to these groups. I went on one trip where I was almost twice as old as everyone else, and although it was fun, I was certainly not in the same headspace as the rest of the group. If you are interested in bird watching and other naturalist activities, fishing, photography or hiking, look for an outfitter that offers trips that fit your interests.

Safety and ethics: What is the ratio of clients to guides? The industry standard is 6:1. Have the guides been certified by an industry training association and what level of first-aid training do they have? Although there are no government guidelines, the commercial sea kayaking industry has training and accreditation programs for guides. Also, does the company seem to have a sense of humour? Humour is a strong indicator that when things go wrong people will deal with situations in a fun and relaxing manner.

Insurance: Companies should have liability insurance, check and see if they do. They are required to have it if they are operating within a Provincial or Federal Park. Expect most companies to ask you to complete a medical history form and sign a liability waiver.

Meals: Here's a big difference that you might want to check out, especially if you like to eat well. Most outfitters put on pretty good feeds, but some go an extra distance. In some cases there's an option to lower your trip cost by preparing one or two meals for the whole group. I have gone on several of these and the experience has been fun and the food good and plentiful. On the other hand, I've talked to friends who are excellent cooks and they went out with a group that cooked mainly instant macaroni and cheese. This wasn't the outfitter's fault, they just got on a trip with the wrong type of cooks.

Trip information: Once you have narrowed down the field, you can ask several tour companies to send you information about the trip you think you would like to take. This information will include gear lists of what they expect you to bring, places to stay before and after the trip, transportation and much more. You can tell quite a bit about a company by how they handle your request for this information.

Day trips: Day trips without having to pack all those camping supplies can be a nice adventure without much bother. They can be instructional learning-to-kayak trips, sightseeing trips or just a day of fun and beauty on the water. By taking an introductory 2 to 4 hour paddle, you know if kayaking is a sport for you and if so, you can take the next step, which is taking a kayak training class or going on a longer kayak camping trip.

Designing your own trip: If you can get a group of six or more people together for a trip, many outfitters are willing to offer you your own special trip. Some outfitters will do this for even smaller groups. This would be to your advantage if you wanted a special theme, to paddle slowly or if you were all great paddlers and wanted to travel fast.

Examples of what's out there:
Pacific Northwest Expeditions gives a trip that is a wonderful experience learning about nature and kayaking. The food is organic, they cook to accommodate vegetarians, and often supplement the meals with fresh caught fish.

Sealegs Kayaks and Marine Adventures supplement their meals by diving for shellfish and other ocean goodies. They emphasize the learning experience and take real joy in working with beginning kayakers as well as with seniors and youth. Guests are well catered to with a lot of personal attention.

Wild Heart Adventures and several other outfitters offer trips to Vargas Island in Clayoquot Sound where you stay in the Vargas Inn and have an incredible crab feed. The group has the Vargas Inn entirely to themselves and staying in the old Inn is like taking a trip back in time.

All in all, most people who take a kayak trip want three things. They want pristine viewscapes, mild exercise and the opportunity to learn about the outdoors. Kayaking is one of the best ways of experiencing these outdoor activities with some soft adventure thrown in.

Motherships and sisterships

When I first saw a mothership ad in a kayak magazine, I immediately thought of "Beam me up Scottie" and Star-trek ship Enterprise. A few years later I sat in my kayak in the waters of Nootka Sound and watched Paul paddle into the rigging and get hoisted up about twenty feet in the air and swung aboard the M.V. Uchuck III. Maybe it wasn't very Trekky, but he was aboard the mothership and as the platform splashed down, I timed my entry.

The platform was a wooden pallet with a metal frame under it and wire rope leading up from each of the four corners. The wire rope went to a central bracket about six feet above the pallet. Paddling on to this sling required that there be enough water over the pallet and enough headroom under the cable arrangement. As the small coastal freighter gently rolled, the pallet would be either too high or too low for a brief moment. I timed my approach to match the roll of the freighter, turned my paddle parallel to the kayak to clear the wire ropes and slightly overshot where I should have stopped. A shout from a crewmember above and a quick tug on the wire rope on my part put me back in position. Before I realized it, I was airborne. My hand shot down to the pallet to stabilize my kayak, but this really wasn't necessary. Thinking back, Paul made it all look so easy, which it really was.

Another mothership experience off Jedediah Island required passing kayaks from the bow of a sailboat mothership to the skipper, who was alongside in his inflatable dinghy. As each kayak reached the water, one of us would transfer from the sailboat, join Cliff in the dinghy and then climb into his or her kayak. Using the paddle across the rear of the cockpit and over the dinghy's pontoon this was a very easy maneuver. Although this is called a "wet launch" the people are supposed to stay dry.

So what are *motherships* in relation to the realm of kayaking? It seems the term is used to describe a whole range of support type vessels. The more basic type of mothership service provides marine transportation for kayaks and kayakers. On the other end of the pendulum, motherships can also provide dry sleeping accommodations, meals, showers and all the comforts of home. In other words, no worries about wet gear, leaking tents and heavily laden kayaks.

In both cases, motherships can take kayakers into wonderful paddling areas that would have taken days to reach by paddling. An added benefit is the elimination of having to kayak open crossings, which are boring and can be dangerous if the weather changes suddenly. For those who are not strong paddlers, motherships provide access to areas that would otherwise be inaccessible. During the off-season when the days are short but beautiful and the nights are cool, a mothership can be an ideal solution to extending your kayak adventuring.

Some motherships are called sisterships. The term sistership is used to describe a support vessel that travels as a supply/safety boat and joins you at your camp. Some outfitters and adventure guides like using sisterships as it eliminates having to pack everything into the holds of the kayaks and allows for more goodies to be brought on the trip. As an added benefit, if the weather gets bad, the sistership can become a mothership and transport the group home.

As we tire of paddling familiar and easily accessible areas, the idea of getting dropped somewhere new and away from the madding crowd becomes appealing. Using a mothership can open up new paddling areas for you at a modest cost if the mothership is BC Ferries, the M.V. Uchuck III or the M.V. Lady Rose. For those who want to reach other areas, the cost is higher, but not unreasonable. Some companies offer a variety of mothership adventures and many offer charters where you set the course. Some motherships are famous restored heritage vessels, while others are beautiful yachts. Many mothership adventure companies offer specialty tours that include activities such as whale watching, bear watching, native culture, forest tours, wildlife photography and much more. Most offer guided kayaking. To locate a mothership or sistership for adventure paddling the waters off Vancouver Island, visit the Easykayaker website at www.easykayaker.com.

Paddling clubs and associations

Kayak clubs provide a forum to meet other paddlers, generate new ideas for trips, and promote safe kayaking. It's a cooperative approach to honing skills, and sharing knowledge and experiences.

Joining a paddling club or association is a very practical way of getting some paddling experience with an added degree of safety. You're still responsible for your own safety, but you'll usually be with some experienced paddlers. Safety in numbers certainly counts when you're on the water in small boats.

Another advantage of being a part of a paddling club is that you get to experience new paddling areas and learn launch sites from people who have paddled those areas. Most clubs offer trips every week or two. Experienced members take turns leading the trips.

The older more established clubs tend to be a mixture of canoe paddlers and kayakers. Many of the trips are fresh water canoe type trips and even the saltwater trips will include some canoes. Kayak-only paddling associations are also becoming popular. Joining a group is often a good way to meet good paddling partners for future non-club outings.

There are club etiquette rules to follow. Each club might be a little different, but they all paddle for the same reasons. Try not to be too noisy or talkative while paddling. Most people paddle for the solo experience even while paddling in a group. Don't paddle too close to another person's kayak or canoe, but try to stay near the group. If you wander too far from the group, the trip leader has a harder time keeping tabs on everyone.

Besides offering day trips and camping adventures, the larger more established clubs often have

- newsletters
- monthly meetings with slide shows or videos
- clinics and workshops
- libraries of kayaking books
- gear rentals of such things as marine radios and ERIRBs
- locator ads for buying and selling used boats and gear

Paddling group size varies by club and tends to range from 6 to 25 paddlers per outing. The larger groups tend to spread out more, as the strong paddlers tend to take off in the lead leaving the slower ones to follow. Many of the smaller clubs are more spontaneous having trips when the members are available and the groups in the smaller clubs usually stick closer together when paddling.

If you're new to paddling, short of paddling partners, want to meet new people or learn new places to paddle, joining a club is a great way to get out on the water and have some fun.

Renting a sea kayak

Most small towns and cities along the east and west coasts of Vancouver Island have kayak rental companies. Rentals are available for either for a few hours, day trips or overnight trips. Most rental companies will require that you have kayaking experience before they will rent a kayak to you. If you aren't an experienced kayaker and/or haven't taken a basic kayaking safety course, they can usually provide you with some basic training at a very reasonable cost.

Not all kayaks are created equal. Kayaks are built to suit different purposes, different sized people, they are made from different materials, and each manufacturer makes many different models. Renting kayaks is a great way to test paddle different makes and models, before you take the plunge into buying your own.

Generally, a rental outfit will assist you in choosing the right boat for you and your planned paddling excursion. The rental company should provide you with the basic kayaking equipment, which will include: PFD (personal flotation device), whistle, sprayskirt, paddle float, paddle (plus one spare paddle per group), throw line and bailer or pump. You should also have a water bottle, proper clothing, sun hat, sunscreen, running shoes/ sandals, sunglasses, and a snack. If you are going any real distance, add a compass and chart to this list.

Before you take off paddling with the kayak, you will be given a few "do's and don'ts" by the rental place as to how to treat their boats. They will include how to launch and land, not to drag the boat on the beach, not to sit on top of the kayak or PFD and what not to do with the paddle. You can usually expect a few skill-testing questions to be thrown into the dialog.

Most rental outfits will allow you to take the kayak on your vehicle to a remote paddling location if that is your desire. They will want you to have sturdy roof racks or foam kayak cradle supports. Many companies will help you with this. They usually prefer you to use tie-down straps instead of rope to secure the kayak while transporting it.

For overnight trips you should check the boat over closely. Examine the cords, the rudder and cable, and any working parts. If the kayak has previously suffered some abuse, bulkheads can start to leak into the storage hatches and soak your food and clothing. For this reason, it's wise to keep items in waterproof bags. You should also consider filing a float plan (available in this book) if you will be off on an extended trip. Camping and equipment lists in this book provide information on what to take and how to pack the kayak.

Many kayak rental outfits advertise their prices on the Internet. Our Easykayaker web site (click Kayak Rentals) lists dozens of rental locations. The price for a day's kayak rental currently averages around $40. The longer you rent the boat the better the price per day becomes. You can also rent by the hour if all you want is a short one or two hour paddle. If you are new to kayaking and want maximum stability in a watercraft, renting a double kayak may be an option and will cost less than renting two singles.

Not all Vancouver Island kayak rental companies have high standards, but most do. Many companies like Sealegs of Ladysmith, sell their rental stock off each year or two, so you are renting relatively new boats in great condition. Rental companies and touring outfitters are good sources when looking to buy a fairly new used kayak at a decent price.

Section 8—The Most Popular Kayaking Area in the World

This section describes launch sites shown on the opposite page. For each location shown on this map there is another detailed map and description of that area, a bit of local history, suggested paddling routes, and our experiences paddling that location.

Gary at Evening Cove
Photo by Marina Sacht

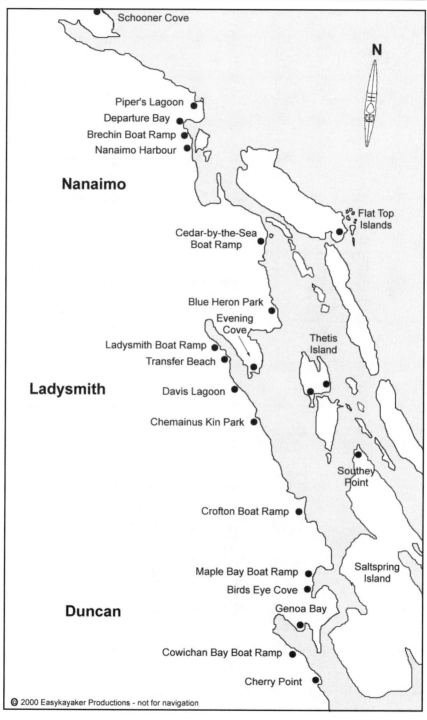

Eastern Vancouver Island Launch Sites

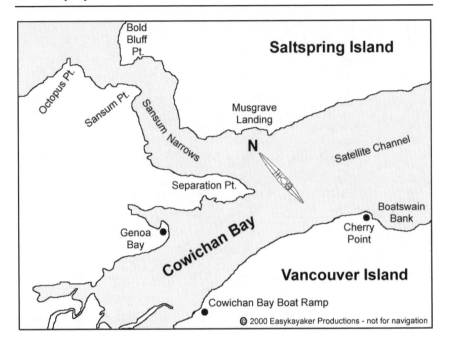

Charts #3441 and #3442
Tidal Reference: Fulford Harbour

Where's my lightning rod?

Cowichan Bay / Genoa Bay / Cherry Point

There are three launch sites for this area that are Easykayaker favourites. The first is the public boat ramp at the west side of the village of Cowichan Bay (aka Cow Bay). There is a small park here, lots of parking, and if the boat ramp is busy, you can launch from the shore. Eco West Adventures has a kayak equipment store nearby and they also rent kayaks, provide instruction and give guided kayak tours from this location.

The second launch site, Genoa Bay, is the location to use if you want to do the trip through Sansum Narrows to Maple Bay. This is an incredibly beautiful paddle, but the current can reach 3 knots in places, so it's not a trip for beginners and you need to time your paddle with the current (floods north, ebbs south). Usually people leave a car at Bird's Eye Cove (south end of Maple Bay) and launch at Genoa Bay or vice versa depending on tides. The distance by road is only 2.5 km but it's a 15 km paddle. The public access at Genoa Bay looks like its part of the Marina, but locals assure me that it is public.

The third launch site is from a Cowichan Regional District Park at Cherry Point. The official name is Cherry Point Nature Observation Park. It's located at the end of Garnett Road, which is off Cherry Point Road. Even though parking is limited to only about 10 vehicles, we've always found plenty of parking available. The shallows in front of the park are named Boatswain Bank. At low tide Boatswain Bank is a great beach for nature observation, but it is also a long but easy walk to the water to launch your kayak. The view toward Saltspring Island is wonderful, but the Vancouver Island side in both directions from Cherry Point is well settled. It's a nice paddle along the shore in either direction, but it isn't a pristine shoreline. Paul and I paddle enough deserted coastlines on other trips that we can enjoy the older settled shores of this area and the picturesque old boathouses, docks and wharves. There is certainly a photo-opt or two along the way.

The area that comprises Cowichan Bay and Genoa Bay offers a variety of paddling conditions and scenery. Cowichan Bay is a large body of open water with its major axis running in an east-west direction. The west end of the bay is a shallow river estuary. Two rivers, the Cowichan and Koksilah, meander around low marshy islands as their many channels enter the bay. An old but still operating mill and log booming grounds are on a manmade island stuck out in the middle of the bay. Halfway up the north coast is an inlet to a small piece of paradise named Genoa Bay. The mouth of Cowichan Bay opens to Satellite Channel and to Sansum Narrows on the north.

Because Cowichan Bay and Cherry Point are open to Satellite Channel, wind can be a problem in this area. The good thing is that waves don't often get the opportunity to build unless the wind is blowing in from Satellite Channel. We've been out on days when the wind would blow the hat off your head and yet the waves are small. If it is windy and you have a high tide, the estuaries are a good place to visit. If you do so, don't go traipsing overland during the nesting season. If you stay in your boats, you won't disturb the birds, but on land you could cause a mother to leave her nest and a gull could gobble up her eggs or babies.

My favourite paddle in these waters was one early summer day. We launched at the Cowichan Bay boat ramp and paddled over to the mill and under some of the wharves. We continued on to Skinner Point and up the coast to Genoa Bay. Along the way we saw a teenage boy playing with his dog on the beach. It turned out to be Michael, who had lived a few doors down from us when he was younger. He had also been one of Paul's students when Paul taught at North Oyster Elementary School. Michael looked more like his dad than the 10-year-old we had each known. We had a short catch up visit with him and then we paddled around the corner into Genoa Bay.

It was a day and night transition from an open body of water with industrial overtones into this serene bay with a quaint little settlement, rolling farmland, one large mountain and one shore of untouched forest. We paddled under a few docks and around the boathouses. Some of the old wooden boats were works of a past art that we see little of today. We followed the west shore up to the wide rolling grasslands at the head of the bay. We could see cattle grazing, but no farm buildings or houses. As we continued our journey around Genoa Bay we passed two kayakers paddling multicoloured plastic kayaks. I asked about the kayaks, as I had never seen any boats quite like that before. It turned out that they had brought the kayaks with them out from Quebec when they moved here.

All along the eastside of the bay uninhabited forest mixed with small grasslands and nice beaches. The land is Indian Reserve or First Nations land and with the exception of one or two floating dwellings close to Separation Point, it is not lived on. We pulled up on one of the beaches and enjoyed our lunch in the sun. As the opening of the bay faces due south, it is usually a warm cheery location if the sun is out. Lunch was our usual fare of honey-garlic pepperoni, cheese bread, trail mix, fruit and fruit juice. I'm sure we had some dessert, but I can't remember what. There's something wonderful about being able to pull up onto a deserted beach on a nice day and leisurely eat a great lunch.

After lunch as we exited Genoa Bay, we met up with one of Eco West's beginning kayak classes. The instructor/guides were giving helpful tips, but by now everyone had caught on and the group seemed to be having a lot of fun. It certainly made me reflect on my first time out kayaking with Wild Heart Adventures. We joined up with Eco West's group for a minute or two to say hi and then headed east toward Separation Point and Sansum Narrows. We enjoyed the scenery, particularly the rocky shoreline and occasional small sandy beaches along the way. The water was deep enough that we could paddle along almost touching the shore. As we came around a rock to a small beach we encountered a Bald Eagle standing on a deer carcass ripping meat from it with its powerful hooked beak. We were less than 15 feet away and the glare we received conveyed the eagle's message quite clearly. We slowly paddled about 20 feet further away trying to send back the message that we were not going to be a threat. The carcass was missing the hide and the main cuts of meat. Some person most likely had shot the deer for food and had made a gift of the carcass to the birds of the area. The pecking order was quite apparent, the eagle was number one, nearby were some hawks and vultures in the trees waiting their turn, slightly further away were the ravens and there was little hope that anything would be left for the crows.

It was hard to pull ourselves away from this marvelous sight of the eagle feeding, but we eventually did and headed out to Separation Point where Cowichan Bay, Satellite Channel and Sansum Narrows all meet. The tide was flooding and at Separation Point there were tidal rapids with small standing waves. Boy did I want to drift into the rapids, but I knew that wasn't the direction we were headed. I decided to paddle the edge of the rapids and then drift into Sansum Narrows. Paul caught up with me and we gazed down the narrows; what a view it was with huge mountains reaching right down to the sea. Across the channel Musgrave Landing on Saltspring Island was calling to me. It was amazing how far into Sansum Narrows we drifted in the minute or two as we discussed the pros and cons of crossing over to Saltspring. Paul's good sense won out and we decided to head across the mouth of Cowichan Bay toward Cherry Point and then turn and catch a free ride on wind and tide back along Cow Bay's southern shore.

It took a couple of minutes of power paddling to loosen Sansum Narrows' grip on us. As it does on many summer afternoons when the land warms, the wind came up but we weren't exposed until about halfway across the bay. The wind and small waves were broadsiding us as we finished the 2 km crossing, but it was a small price to pay as we were soon surfing the waves down Cowichan Bay. I wish I had had my GPS with me to clock the speeds we were traveling. We were astonished how quickly we traveled the south shore. At this point we didn't want our trip to end, so we paddled in and out of some of the marinas looking at the boats and the old ramshackled buildings.

When we got back to the boat launch, it was in use, so we paddled past and landed at the grassy park. We had gotten splashed a few times crossing Cow Bay and we took advantage of the picnic table to spread our gear out to dry while we finished off the dregs from our earlier lunch. For only having paddled about 12 km, we had seen and experienced many different types of landscapes and paddling conditions. On the way home, we drove part way up Mount Sicker and gathered some interesting rocks for Paul to use in his teaching.

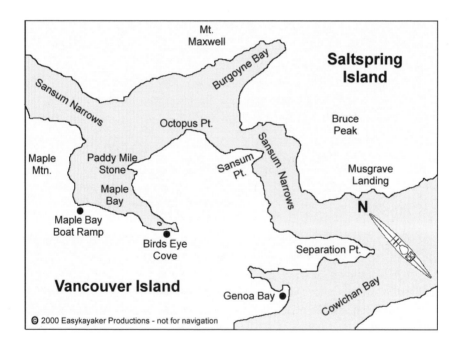

Chart #3442
Tidal Reference: Fulford Harbour

Maple Bay boat ramp

We have two favourite Maple Bay area launch sites. One is a small, road right-of-way in Bird's Eye Cove. If you drive along the bay on Genoa Bay Road, just south of Maple Bay Marina you will find a grassed access to launch your kayaks. You can back into the right-of-way, between two houses, and unload your boats and gear. After unloading, a short drive is required to find a place where the road is wide enough to park. This launch site is just south of Chisholm Island and the cove beyond the island is shallow and will turn into mud flats at low tide. You should check your tide tables for your launch and return times.

Another easy location to launch from is the Maple Bay boat ramp. As you come down the road from Duncan, turn left onto Beaumont Avenue and follow the road just past a small store. You will soon notice the trailer parking on the left. Turn right into the wide ramp area.

The area of Maple Bay, Sansum Narrows and Saltspring Island's West Coast bring a special type of geographical experience. You're sitting in your kayak east of Paddy Mile Stone staring down Sansum Narrows. Suddenly, you feel very diminutive as though you exist in an ocean microcosm. Maple Mountain (535 m) northeast of Maple Bay, looms over Arbutus Point. In mid-summer, bands of Scotch broom mark the huge towering hill with their bright yellow flowers. Across the narrows the steep bluffs of Mount Maxwell on Saltspring Island (595 m) help create the sense of a coastal fiord. For a moment you wonder if you're kayaking in the fjords of Norway.

Today we were on a family outing to visit Maple Bay's annual Classic Wooden Boat show and then to show our families and friend, Barb, what we call the moonsnail beach. The Wooden Boat Association features their crafts in shows at different marinas along the coast. It's an interesting way to spend a couple of hours. We would have seen more of the show by land, but we were content to paddle by the boats and view them from the water.

We launched from the Maple Bay boat ramp and headed toward Bird's Eye Cove. Gary, his daughter, Katherine, and friend Barb, were in singles. My wife and son were in a double kayak and I was in my Storm kayak. A light, spring breeze blew as we followed the coastline to the docks near Bird's Eye Cove. We maneuvered between the docks and shore, under ramps, pipes and cables, all the way to Chisholm Island and around the island. Usually, we can get through all the narrow openings without hindrance.

Next we paddled through the boat show admiring the old Chriscrafts, wooden sloops and ketches, and various old, wooden tugs and ships. Once we had taken in our fill of teak decks, oak gunwales, and a variety of antique engines we quickly paddled across to the west shore of Bird's Eye Cove and headed toward Paddy Mile Stone.

As we neared Paddy Mile Stone, we felt the winds blowing through Sansum Narrows. We have experienced windless days in this area, but today wasn't to be one of them. We paddled around Paddy Mile Stone and headed toward Arbutus Point. Our destination was the moonsnail beach, a flat section of shore about ¾ km before Octopus Point. With so many shells and moonsnails this beach has always held our interest and keeps us revisiting it.

Our paddle along this section was a little rough but okay for a family. The winds were largely from the Northwest and creating slightly rough conditions. We were working hard enough to create a good appetite for a beach lunch. Soon we were coasting into the wind-swept, shell-laden beach.

After lunch we explored the beach for quite a distance toward Octopus Point. The children wanted to search an unoccupied cabin. It was rather dilapidated and lonely-looking but we explained that it was someone's private property. Both kids understood quickly and wandered off somewhere else. After our beach scavenging we started kayaking back to Paddy Mile Stone. We paddled into the winds for about 20 minutes until we reached the huge boulder on the point. Once we were in Maple Bay the winds settled (we were also in the lee of Maple Mountain which was likely sheltering us from the winds). We paddled more casually, chatted, and socialized with each other. Kayaking has a lot of intrinsic benefits like providing premium chatting time with friends and family while getting light exercise at the same time.

After the gear was packed away and the boats tied to the trailer, the adults had a light drink on the Maple Bay Pub's deck overlooking the water. Katherine and Jordan, twelve and thirteen, played on the beach underneath the pub. Barb and I talked about the late 60's and early 70's on Vancouver Island. It was fun reminiscing about the 'old' days. The happy smiles of adults and children alike were evidence that our day of kayaking had been enjoyable to all.

Moonsnail Footnote:

The moonsnail is unique to the coast with its large shell, gigantic foot, and unusual egg structure. I've heard the foot can be almost a foot square and can be carved into snail steaks for food. The plunger-shaped egg formation left in an inter-tidal zone is very unusual. When you first kayak or canoe over one you're completely intrigued with the shape. In fact the moonsnail's eggs, numbering in the thousands, are sandwiched between sand layers and glued together with its mucus. The moonsnail travels beneath the sand searching for clams and oysters. When it finds its prey, a small hole is drilled and the bivalve is sucked out.

Moonsnail - actual size

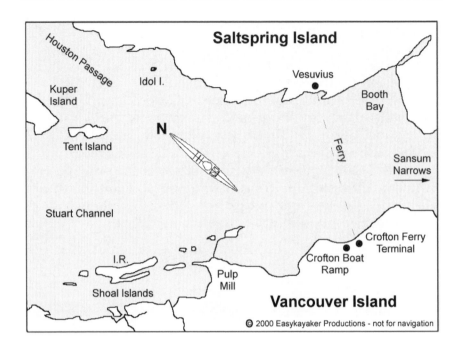

Chart #3442
Tidal Reference: Fulford Harbour

Leo among the Shoal Islands

Crofton boat ramp

Crofton is a small community south of Chemainus. A pulp mill on the north overshadows the town, but for most of Crofton's visitors, the town is where you catch the ferry to Saltspring Island. On the north side next to the ferry dock is a boat ramp, which is the only easy launch site that we have found in this area. It's a great launch site with the exception that it can get quite busy during long weekends in the summer.

Although the Crofton pulp mill doesn't offer the kind of scenery most paddlers enjoy, it does create an environment that attracts wildlife. Usually when we paddle this area, we see large numbers of seals, sea lions, great blue herons and bald eagles.

My first paddle from this launch site was with Brian, a longtime friend, in the yellow double. Just after launching we saw water being splashed about six feet into the air. The splashing was a five-minute paddle away from us and continued as we paddled toward it. We were both speculating what was causing the splashing as we closed the distance. Once we were close we could tell that it was three or four seals playing a rough and tumble game with each other. One of the seals came shooting straight up out of the water next to our boat and was completely airborne looking down at us with an expression on his face that clearly indicated he hadn't planned on seeing us there.

After visiting with the seals, we headed north on the outside of the mill booming grounds, paddled by the sea lions basking on the round cylinder shaped floats and headed along Stuart Channel into the Shoal Islands. This is a magical place that I never tire of visiting. The Shoal Islands encompass a flat estuary that is hundreds of acres in size and protected from wind. Other than the mill, which you don't see because it's behind you, there is little sign of mankind.

There are several considerations when going into this area, first the tide must be at least seven feet or preferably higher. Paul and I have carried our boats through the thick oozing flats on lower tides and quickly discovered how tiresome even two hundred metres of slogging can be.

Secondly, much of the land in this area is owned by First Nations. Unfortunately, there have been pot hunters disturbing grave sites. The area should be treated with respect. Lastly, it is an estuary for Bonsal Creek and the Chemainus River so it is bird habitat and the nesting birds shouldn't be disturbed. If we enter the area during the spring/summer nesting season, we stay closer to the Shoal Islands and away from the many mouths of the creek and river.

We usually have lunch on the small Island north of Willy Island and then paddle back on the outside of the Shoal Islands. If the tide is still high enough we like to cut in just before the mill and paddle under the causeway bridge into the mill booming area (if there isn't active booming work in progress). This short cut saves a lot of distance and if the booming ground is idle, it's a great place to see wildlife. Maybe I've been in the bush too long, but I do find the mill interesting when I'm paddling by it.

On another trip we started out from Crofton on an ebbing tide and paddled with the gentle current south from Stuart Channel into Sansum Narrows. Our plan was to have lunch around 12:30 and then head back on the flood tide. We followed the west shore and examined some sea caves, a fish farm and a huge old boat moored in one of the coves. We then crossed over to Saltspring (about 1 km) and found a nice beach just north of Burgoyne Bay for lunch and explored a couple of sea caves on foot.

During this leg of the journey Michael Dean took a photo of me paddling my purple and yellow Solstice GT. I scanned this photo and used it as a desktop image for my computer. A few months later, Michael surprised me with a watercolour that he painted from this photo.

On the way back we followed Saltspring's shore. We were going to cross back over to the Vancouver Island side at the north end of the narrows, but it was such a nice day that we headed to Saltspring's Booth Bay. The bay has an inlet that I wanted to visit, but the tide was still too low. We carried on most of the way to Vesuvius before turning toward Crofton.

We could have walked on the ferry with our kayaks at Vesuvius and returned home that way but we decided to paddle the 5 km crossing. We had covered about 22 km by the time we reached the end of this long crossing. The only excitement on the crossing was the passing ferry. The ferry throws a fun wake that is real easy to surf or fun to take head on.

All in all, the Crofton area is a nice place to paddle. Sansum Narrows is easy to paddle if you're paddling with the tide. We haven't encountered any dangerous tidal rapids and the only hazard is boat traffic, which we've never had much of a problem with, due to the width of both the channel and the narrows.

Taken on another day and a few kilometres to the north of Crofton, we encountered a sailboat race suffering from lack of wind. Like the tortoise and the hare story, the tortoise (kayakers) won.

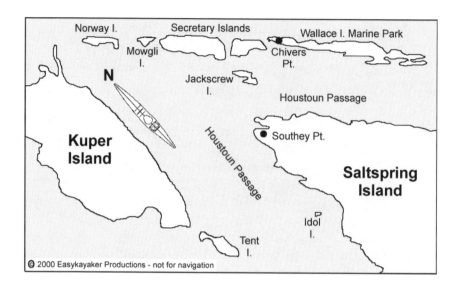

Chart #3442
Tidal Reference: Fulford Harbour

Photo by Marina Sacht

Southey Point—Saltspring Island

This launch site is easy to find, just take any of the three roads that go to the northern end of Saltspring Island. If you want a road map, you can usually get one at the ferry terminal. Windermere Saltspring Realty also produces a good road map for Saltspring. Once you get to the northern tip of the Island, you'll come to Southey Point Road. Off Southey is Arbutus Road, and at the end of Arbutus is the type of beach and access that we at Easykayaker love. You can drive right down to the gently sloping beach and the beach surface is very smooth. The only downside is that the turn around is poor and parking is almost nonexistent right at the beach. These are minor problems unless you have a trailer full of kayaks.

For several years my work had taken me to Saltspring Island once or twice a month. I often had spare time between appointments and before catching ferries home. Most of this time and my lunch breaks were spent exploring Saltspring's parks and beach accesses. Although there are many great paddling spots, the area of Walker Hook, Wallace Island, Jackscrew Island and the Secretary Islands really intrigued me.

My work mainly consisted of inspecting completed residential energy retrofit renovations and this brought me in contact with many old time local residents, most of whom I pumped for launch site information. Unfortunately none of these people were paddlesports enthusiasts, and many expressed the thought that I was plumb crazy to want to go out in Houstoun Passage in a tiny kayak. Finally, I talked to some fellow kayakers that put me onto Southey Point as the best launch site for the northwest end of Saltspring Island.

There are many paddling route options from Southey Point. The coastline in both directions is interesting, especially in the southern direction where you paddle by the very small but intriguing Idol Island (about 3 km). I've read that Idol Island was used by the First Nations people as a location to place their dead, as Coffin Island was used further north near Yellow Point.

Another paddling option is to head over to Tent Island and Kuper

Island (see section for Chemainus launch site). Tent and Kuper are First Nations land and most of the coastline is unsettled and quite beautiful.

My favourite option is to paddle to Wallace Island and the Secretary Chain (Wallace, Jackscrew, North & South Secretary, Mowgli and Norway Islands). Most of Wallace is a provincial marine park. It has good campsites and hiking trails. The rest of the islands are private property with non-welcoming signs.

Wallace Island is a divided island. The kayakers mainly take to the north end at Chivers Point and the motor and sailboats go to Conover Cove on the south end. It takes about an hour to walk the length of the Island on an old road, which is now a nice trail. If you want to read more about Wallace Island, David Conover wrote two books about what it was like to live there during his twenty or so years on the island. They are titled *One Man's Island* and *Once Upon an Island*.

Great Horned Owl photo by Gary Dobrovolsky

Houstoun Passage between Wallace and Saltspring has a bad habit of getting windy in the afternoon during the summer, but the waves aren't usually too big. The crossing is just under one kilometre from Southey Point to Jackscrew (10 minutes or less) and only once in this area have we had to deal with much chop. From Jackscrew on you can avoid open water and paddle in the shelter of the many islands.

There's a great little cove for swimming with a beautiful sandy beach on the west side of Jackscrew Island. This cove is well protected, even on a windy day. One day as we paddled in for our swim, we witnessed some kayaks floating out of the cove. The owners had left them too close to the water and the rising tide cast them adrift. We gave the kayak owners a

Photo by Marina Sacht

shout and herded their boats toward them.

In general, currents are minor in the entire area. On flood (rising) tides they flow north and on ebb (falling) tides the currents flow south. Just off both the tips of Southey Point and Penetakut Spit there are minor tidal rapids, which look exciting on a flat calm day, but really won't give much of a thrill. When it's a little choppy out, you don't even see or feel the current unless you stop paddling and drift through it.

We would day-paddle this area more often if it were not for having to catch a ferry to either Thetis or Saltspring. It's a wonderful paddling location that I doubt we would tire of. Most of our future paddles here will probably be overnighters, eliminating the need for taking a ferry. Evening Cove, Ladysmith, Chemainus and Crofton launch sites are all within a day's paddle of the campsites on Wallace and Tent Islands.

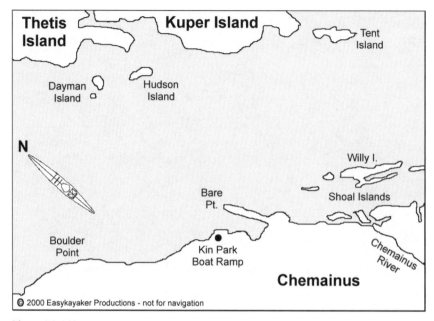

Chart #3442
Tidal Reference: Fulford Harbour

Just off Kin Park

Chemainus' Kin Park

The launch site recommended by Easykayaker for the Chemainus area is at Kinsman Park. This launch site gets "two paddles up" for ease of access, good parking, a great beach to launch from, a boat ramp and for being a nice little waterfront park. To find Kinsman Park, follow Chemainus Road to Oak Street (look for Thetis Island Ferry signs and follow them), make a left onto Maple Street and drive to the waterfront. The park is located at the intersection of Maple Street and Esplanade Street.

There are three choices for paddling routes. You can head north toward Ladysmith, south toward Crofton or straight across to Thetis, Kuper and Tent Islands.

Choice 1

Heading north toward Ladysmith you can stay in shallow water and enjoy watching the seafloor. There aren't many inlets and coves to explore, but there are nice pebble and sand beaches. This area is quite built-up, so you will see many homes along the shore and most likely have a chance to visit with beachcombers as you paddle by. The only landmarks are Boulder Point and Davis Lagoon (see section on Davis Lagoon launch site). Boulder Point isn't really a point and the boulder isn't very large, but it's the only boulder on the beach for miles in either direction. There is a public beach access at the boulder from the end of South Oyster School Road, but I wouldn't want to carry a kayak down those steep stairs.

Choice 2

If you choose instead to paddle south toward Crofton, you will cross Chemainus Bay and pass by Bare Point. Bare Point is an industrial area. Just past the point is the abandoned BC Hydro Georgia Basin Generating Station. Built in the early and mid 1950s, it was the world's largest oil fueled generating plant at the time and was capable of supplying electricity for all of Vancouver Island. It was only operational for about ten years. The generating equipment was removed and sold many years ago. This paddling route has many contrasts to the one heading toward Ladysmith. The water here is deep, even near the shore, there are few beaches or landing sites until just before the Shoal Islands, and there is very little development along the shore.

This my favourite direction to paddle from Chemainus if the tide is high, as the area inside the Shoal Islands is well worth visiting (see the

Crofton launch site section for more information regarding paddling the Shoal Islands). One early fall day with a very high tide (12 ft.), five of us paddled into this area and up the north fork of the Chemainus River and then down the south fork. There was no current, and we felt we were in another world. Big juicy blackberries hung over the water in places and we were able to feast on them from the cockpits of our kayaks.

Choice 3

If you choose to paddle across to Thetis, Kuper and Tent Islands from Kinsman Park, it's a 4 ½ km crossing to Hudson or Dayman Island and then just a short distance to Thetis or Kuper. If you're heading to Tent Island, it is just over a 5 km crossing from Bare Point.

Paul and I had a great opportunity present itself one day when our wives decided to go to Saltspring Island for the day. We talked them into dropping us off at Chemainus and we planned to paddle over and meet them at Saltspring's Southey Point. Our intended paddling route was to head over to Hudson Island, along Kuper's west shore, then over to Tent for lunch and a hike. After our hike we planned to paddle to Southey Point to explore Saltspring's shoreline. Things don't always go as planned.

We got dropped off at Kinsman Park in Chemainus and launched from the boat ramp with some difficulty. It was windy and whitecapping right at the boat ramp. This area is usually sheltered, but the wind was coming from the wrong direction that day. Trying to get into a kayak that is bobbing up and down in breaking waves requires a keen sense of timing. I got splashed by waves and almost did a wet-exit before I was in and paddling out far enough from shore to do up my sprayskirt. The waves weren't too high, but the water looked dark and angry. The weather forecast was for the winds to diminish around noon. It was 10 A.M. I decided that I didn't want to do a crossing the way the water looked. We decided to follow the shoreline north instead and hoped that weather conditions would improve. We got to the most northerly Shoal Island and had the choice of going way out to get around log booms or to cut inside where it would be sheltered. We couldn't quite see how far out the log booms extended, but we could see dark seas and many whitecaps out there. We decided to go inside and were rewarded with beautiful paddling conditions. The only catch was that the tide was falling and this whole inside area goes dry very quickly.

We found out just how quickly. Within minutes, we had a view of 4 km of mudflats before us and about ¾ km of mudflats behind us. This wasn't really a surprise, as we knew when we planned the paddle that this route wouldn't be an option due to the very low tides that day. At this point I thought we might end up paddling to Crofton later in the day and meeting our wives there on their return to Vancouver Island. Fortunately both parties had cell phones and we could easily deviate from our prearranged plans.

We were now sitting high and dry on mudflats. Time to see how soft and slippery it was going to be. There was no water in sight, only what looked to be a long walk. The mud wasn't too soft until we picked up the boats. The added weight of two boats made us sink a little deeper, and boy was it slippery. We started with Paul carrying both bows and me carrying both sterns. It wasn't too long before we switched and left one boat behind. I was starting to regret bringing so much extra gear and food along. We had only gone about half a kilometre when we came across a small stream that had been hidden from view. Because it was recessed into the mudflats we didn't see it until we were almost in it. Talk about smiling faces. We went back for the other kayak and soon had both boats at the stream (which was really part of the Chemainus River).

We were pretty well mud splattered as we reached the stream. The water wasn't deep enough to paddle in, but we could now tow the boats easily. There was almost no current. Several times the water deepened and we had to get into the kayaks for a short paddle until the stream became shallow again. We had to go quite a ways outside of Willy Island to get away from the mudflats, but by then the wind was dying down and Paul thought conditions looked good enough for a crossing to Tent Island. The insides of the kayaks were the muddiest I'd ever seen them.

The crossing was about 3 ½ km of rock 'n' roll, but conditions improved as we neared Tent Island. During lunch on the island, the weather turned into what I can only describe as perfect. It was sunny and warm (t-shirt and shorts weather) with little wind. Being one of the lowest tides of the year, the beachcombing was fabulous between Tent and Kuper (which were now joined due to the low tide). We decided to hike all the way around Tent Island, but halfway down the west side of the island, the trail and beach disappeared. We then bushwacked our way across the centre of the island to the east side. On the east side we crossed a beach covered in millions of sand dollars. We actually had to take quite a detour to avoid walking on them.

After the sand dollars, we found a nice spot and sat down for a relaxing lunch. After lunch we had a visit with a couple whose sailboat was moored nearby. We always seem to meet interesting people in unusual places. The couple had been gathering oysters and clams for supper. The husband decided to try a raw oyster. I probably shuddered. It's been a while since I've eaten one raw and it will be even longer before I do it again!

With a rendezvous time we wanted to stick to, we were soon back paddling. We had a 2 km crossing to Saltspring in water that was quite flat. Just past Southey Point there were minor tidal rapids. I had been to Saltspring many times and had traveled the Island extensively always on the lookout for good launch sites. The coves on both sides of Southey Point were the best I'd found for this end of the Island. The only problem is that it had been a while and I had only viewed the area from the land and at a much higher tide.

We expected to see our wives on shore waving to us, but unknown to us they were a bit behind schedule. We ended up going by what I thought was Southey Point and down the shoreline of Saltspring—it was quite a nice trip. Jackscrew and Wallace Islands loomed ahead, but we finally decided we should give Teesh and Imelda a call to see where they were. I landed on a pebble beach and retrieved the cell phone from the front hatch. They were running late, but the good news was that they had had a sushi making demonstration and had bought the supplies and matt for making sushi.

We headed back and explored both coves at Southey Point and landed at the end of Arbutus Road (see section on Southey Point launch site). The sushi that night was great!

A few things to note. Watch for the ferry to Thetis. It throws quite a wake, which we love to surf. Kuper, Tent and some of the Shoal Islands are First Nations land. If you're planning on camping on Tent Island, you should phone the Penelakut Band Council office at (250) 246-2321 during business hours to request permission. At one time Tent Island was leased by the Penelakut Band to the BC Government for use as a park. It is still used by many boaters although the lease expired years ago.

Photo by Marina Sacht

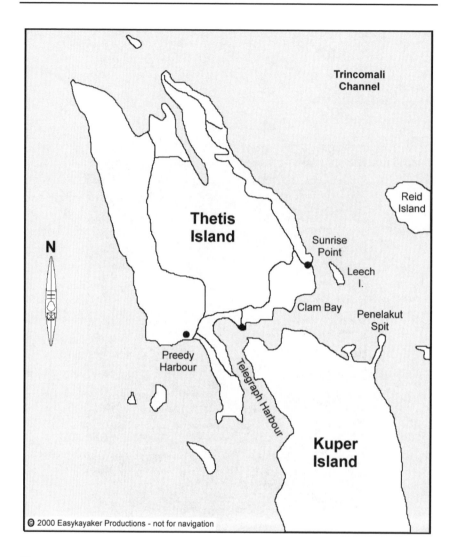

Charts #3442 and #3443
Tidal Reference: Fulford Harbour

Thetis Island

Our favourite method of paddling this area is to take the ferry over to Thetis Island, launch from one of the three good launch sites and take advantage of the wonderful restaurant/pub while waiting for the return ferry. The ferry to Thetis departs from Chemainus' old town section at the bottom of Oak Street. You can check the ferry schedule by going to www.easykayaker.com. You should arrive at the ferry at least 15 minutes before sailing. I haven't encountered a full ferry going over, but I have on the way back (when the Capernwray Bible Camp ends one of their sessions). Some ferry trips go non-stop, others are a bit slower as they stop at Kuper Island. Look for seals on the reefs around Preedy Harbour during the ferry ride.

Most crossings are boring, not much to look at, you seem to move slowly and usually the other side of the crossing doesn't appear any closer after 15 minutes of paddling. Most kayakers will agree that the kayak excels as the perfect craft to explore the intertidal zone. In my mind, if you like deep water, your vessel of choice should be a sailboat.

Unfortunately, most interesting kayak adventures require crossings.

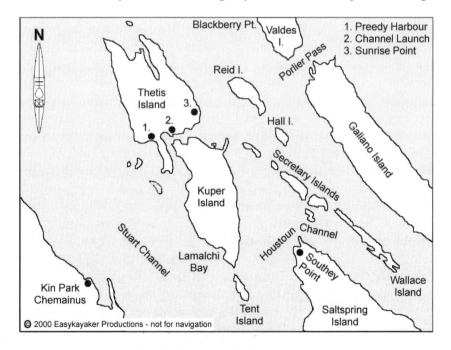

© 2000 Easykayaker Productions - not for navigation

The Thetis Island launch sites are notable exceptions to this. Although you can paddle to Thetis Island from Blue Heron Park, Evening Cove or Kin Park (Chemainus), it will add about two hours roundtrip for the crossing time and that two hours could be better spent exploring some incredible coastline.

The first Thetis launch site is next to the ferry dock in Preedy Harbour (on the north side of the dock). We use this site when we want to save money as a walk-on ferry passenger. One of us will grab a kayak bow in each hand and the other the two sterns. This is the easiest way for two people to carry two kayaks. As the sterns are heavier, we load our food and extra gear in the front hatches. Having a set of kayak wheels makes walking onto the ferry much easier. Once you walk onto Thetis, you'll see a nice easy short trail down to a sandy, gravelly beach on the left. This launch site is good at any tide.

Our favourite paddle from the ferry launch site is to head south to Telegraph Cove, go through the channel between Thetis and Kuper Islands and out to Clam Bay or Penelakut Spit. It was on this short paddle that I first tried towing two kayaks at the same time (but that's another story—see the section on kayaking for kids). This is also a good launch site for going around Thetis Island, but it's about 17 km around and much more if you explore all the ins and outs of North Cove (the 3 km long inlet is quite interesting at a high tide).

A canal between Thetis and Kuper Islands is a second launch site. As you drive off the Thetis ferry, go straight (i.e. don't take the first right which goes to the restaurant/pub) for a short distance and take the right fork called Pilkey Point Road and drive a short distance toward Clam Bay. Take the second right off Pilkey Point Road onto a gravel road called Marina Road—look for the "Public Access to Beach" sign. You can drive to within a stones throw from the water. The trail is very short but steep for about six feet. At low tide launching is muddy and slippery. We have launched here to paddle Norway, Mowgli and the Secretary Islands or to go around Kuper Island and to visit Tent Island. We have also used this launch site to go on overnight trips to Wallace Island, Saltspring Island and to Blackberry Point on Valdes Island. After unloading your boats and gear, park your car outside of the turn around area as per the parking signs.

Our favorite Thetis launch site is at the end of Sunrise Point Road, just inside Leech Island. From the ferry you go straight, right on Pilkey Point Road and then across the island until you take another right on Sunrise Point Road. Sunrise Point Road ends at an easily accessed gently sloping beach. Once unloaded, you have to drive back up the hill a hundred metres or so to find parking. Not only is this the easiest beach access, but it's a nice beach at any tide and has a gorgeous view of many islands. We like paddling this area because most of it is uninhabited. Sometimes the water is so clear you can see down 10 metres and the coastline is also very interesting. You can island hop with very short crossings.

Some things to note are the very minor (but can look scary to the beginner) tidal rapid waves of the tip of Penelakut Spit, the native village on Kuper Island just south of the spit, and how shallow the water is on the east side of Kuper Island. Kuper Island is 99% First Nations land (Indian Reserve #7). Mary Ann Snowden in her book *Island Paddling* tells much of the history of this and other local islands.

Paul and I launched one early spring day from the canal launch site for a paddle around Kuper Island. We headed west and then south around the island counterclockwise. The currents usually run clockwise around Kuper Island, but we didn't know that then. Paddling conditions were ideal; the water was like glass. The weather forecast was good for the entire day. I started talking to Paul about writing a book of our own for the laid-back paddler; Paul started talking about doing it as a website. Soon we were talking about both a book and website, which would both become *Easykayaker*.

Mary Ann Snowden's book mentioned that this area normally has calm wind conditions during the summer, but can be subject to southeasters blowing in from Stuart and Trincomali Channels. This was really not summer, but early spring. Before we were half way down Kuper, the wind came racing out Stuart Channel enough to make me turn my hat around so it wouldn't blow off. Now one of the advantages of this area is that there are a lot of sheltered paddling areas. However, this is only an advantage if your mind isn't made up that you want to go to a certain windy location, which we did. Today the south tip of Kuper Island had the roughest conditions of anywhere in this general area. We bucked good-sized whitecaps hitting us about 15 degrees off our starboard bows. We pulled into Lamalchi Bay for a look around and to rest from the wind and waves. After a nice walk on the beach, we beat it around the corner to Tent Island. We had planned to go around Tent Island, but it was just too rough to be fun.

Tent Island is also First Nations land. Years ago it was leased from the band by the provincial government as a park. It's a favourite visiting place for picnicking and camping by boaters, however it is private land and the rights of the landowners should be respected. We had a nice lunch and hike during which we debated if we should continue around the east side of

Kuper. The east side looked rougher than the way we had come as it was exposed to both Trincomali and Stuart Channels. By the time we were ready to launch the wind had slowed enough for me to turn my hat back around and the only whitecaps were far out into the channels.

Paul and I decided to stay with our original plan and complete the Kuper Island circumnavigation. Soon after launching the wind picked up again, hitting our sterns at about 30 degrees, pushing us toward shore. This is a very flat shore and we kept finding ourselves in shallow water. Great Blue Herons lined the shore about 100 metres apart. It almost seemed that they had used a tape measure to position themselves they were so evenly spaced. Most were fishing, standing in the water on their long stilt-like legs. A short distance before Penelakut Spit we saw a heron up ahead standing on our left (the island was on our right). This was definitely a sign that the water in that area was shallow. We turned hard to the right, paddled to deep water and then rode the wind and waves around the spit into the calm waters of Clam Bay. We had enjoyed a peaceful kayak ride back to the launch site. While sitting in the car waiting for the ferry, it started to rain and then it started to really pour. Fortunately we had had mostly sun and no rain while paddling, which left us feeling rather good after all about the day's weather.

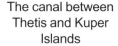

The canal between Thetis and Kuper Islands

Thetis Island Ferry at Crofton

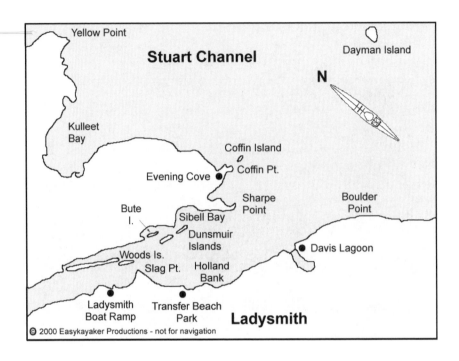

Chart #3443
Tidal Reference: Fulford Harbour

Dunsmuir Islands

Davis Lagoon—south of Ladysmith

Davis Lagoon is just south of Ladysmith on Chemainus Road. This road, which winds along the coastline was the old Island Highway until 1957. The Town of Ladysmith now has three sets of traffic lights. They got their first set of traffic lights around 1975. When you're traveling on the Island highway head for the traffic lights at the south end of town. On the inland side is Davis Road, Dairy Queen and Coronation Mall which houses restaurants like McDonald's and Ricky's. At the lights turn onto Chemainus Road (toward the water). The road bends immediately to the right—follow it for a few kilometres.

Davis Lagoon passes under a bridge and its large flat tidal waters are quite noticeable on your right. As you drive along the old highway you're quite close to the water; you'll know the bridge is approaching as the road turns tight to the left and down a small hill. Pull off immediately just past the bridge. You'll see a short boat launch into the tidal flats. You can launch from either side of the road. If the is tide out, your choice will be obvious. This is not a great launch site at a low tide of less than five feet.

We've launched from Davis Lagoon a few times. This time we hit the tide perfectly, launching and landing. We always wanted to explore the flats fully (they're not big) and our first opportunity now awaited us.

Gary and I quickly untied our kayaks at the short boat launch. We had to be fairly quick—a small truck waited with a speedboat on a trailer. Launching was quick and easy with the high tide. A glimpse of sun warmed the early fall air. We were soon gliding quietly under the bridge toward Stuart Channel.

The winds picked up slightly and were against us as we paddled away from shore. We often choose to paddle into the wind on our way out and return with the wind at our backs (occasionally, we paddle into the wind on our way out and due to a change in wind direction, also paddle into the wind on the way back—sometimes life isn't fair!!). Today we were headed south toward Boulder Point.

Most kayak trips are along uninhabited coastline or the houses are concealed from your view. The houses along this area are easily visible from shore. The first sign of civilization was a group of teens blasting a rock 'n' roll song from their convulsed stereo system—the speakers obviously couldn't handle the volume and shuddered like a swimmer after a polar dip in sea water. Fortunately, we paddled by quickly to a long-range thump from a popular tune.

What I love about this particular paddle is the abundance of sand dollars embedded in the flat, sandy bottom. After experiencing a walk along Parksville beach (and noticing only a few sand dollars) you feel as though you've struck wealth. Because the sand dollars are so abundant here, the water darkens from little light being reflected off the ocean floor. The bottom positively intrigues me—it's fun exploring and we all deserve to be kids!

We alighted at Boulder Point. The day was slightly chilly and we brought out a typical kayak lunch filled with goodies. Boulder Point has beach access from a set of wooden stairs. The beach is a favourite hideout of local Chemainus people. In the summer children can be seen splashing in the water while their parents stretch out and keep a watchful eye. The view of Ladysmith Harbour and Stuart Channel is exquisite. It's a quiet and relaxing place neighbouring a small community area.

We've paddled this part of the coast often. Gary's daughter, Katherine, and my son, Jordan, often accompany us. Both children were now 12 years old and had become sophisticated quickly. Katherine liked short bursts of speed, and often challenged Jordan for a quick race. Both kids have become avid kayakers and outdoors people.

Today, the clouds blocked the sun often enough that the air chilled us. We're smart enough not to pretend we're tough and we decided against paddling further south. While this trip is amidst civilization there's still an abundance of seabirds and occasionally other wildlife about. Also, you can look at the variety of buildings littering the coastline, some are quite unique, while others look like rundown historical landmarks.

This was a short 2-hour trip with about 4 km of lazy paddling. We were soon back at Davis Lagoon. While the tide was slightly lower than when we had launched, Davis Lagoon was still flooded. We ventured into the tidal flats and explored the little channels, our boats skimming only inches off the bottom of the lagoon. Apparently, an old trail to the Holland Creek Falls starts near the end of the flats though we couldn't see any markings or sign of it. Perhaps on another day we'll look for the trail from land.

We paddled to the short boat launch and stepped onto the squishy bottom. The cold water rushing into our diving boots reminded us that the season was changing. We scooted onto shore and loaded our boats. Another relaxing outing at Davis Lagoon.

Sand Dollar Footnote:

The intertidal zone is the area between the splashes at high tides and where the water recedes to at the lowest tides. This area can be divided into four subzones, the spray, high, medium and low intertidal zones.

Sand Dollars need to be right side up and therefore usually live in low intertidal and subtidal zones so that they can avoid being turned over by wave action. They normally live clustered in groups. They are of separate sexes and group living helps reproduction as both the eggs and sperm are discharged to mix at random. Breeding normally takes place during the summer months and the larvae are free swimming. Once they take adult form, they settle to the bottom.

Adult Sand Dollars normally stick in the sand at an angle, with one third or more of their shells buried into the sand. This allows the spines on the underside to catch plankton and algae. Cilia and tube feet move the food to the hole in the center of the shell's bottom side (the mouth). At low tide Sand Dollars will often dig themselves under the sand to prevent being turned over by tidal currents. To protect against being turned over, small Sand Dollars will also ingest heavy sand grains to give them extra weight.

Live Sand Dollars are covered with dark purple-black fur-like spines. The dead Sand Dollars are usually bleached white and missing their spines. The five pedal designs on their topside (back) are from the tiny holes that their tubular feet emerge out of.

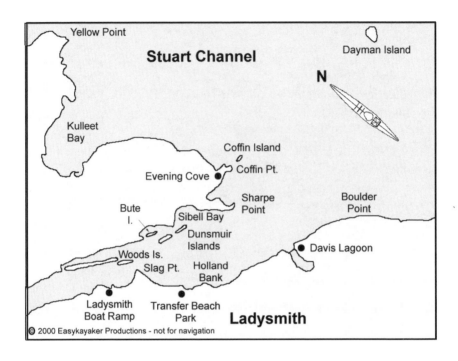

Chart #3443
Tidal Reference: Fulford Harbour

Transfer Beach, Ladysmith

Transfer Beach Park—Ladysmith

Finding Transfer Beach is easy. Ladysmith has three traffic lights. The middle one is where Roberts Street on the west and Transfer Beach Blvd. on the east intersect the Island Highway. Turn at the light and either go shopping for sunscreen or go kayaking, depending on which way you turned. The turnoff is well marked. Ladysmith and Transfer Beach are nice places to visit even if you aren't kayaking.

Ladysmith's waterfront Transfer Beach Park is a great place to bring the family once you have purchased your first kayak. There's a playground, restrooms and a concession stand, so the kids can play while mom and dad take turns trying out the new boat. You can also rent kayaks here from Sealegs Kayaks & Marine Adventures.

For those who want to take a course in kayaking, this is a location to do it with costs as low as $10 to $30 for a two-hour introduction and $90 for a basic course. You can also go to the park and watch an introductory course for free, to see if you might be interested. I've enjoyed watching people taking this course. Usually, you'll see people of all ages and often a parent and child together learning the basics while sitting on the grass with a paddle in their hands. Next the instructors carry the kayaks into the shallow water and help people into the boats. Younger children usually end up in the front seat of a double with a parent in the rear cockpit.

Paul and I don't often launch from Transfer beach for two reasons. First, it's a long distance to carry the boats to the water and secondly, there are usually people watching you, so if you put on your spray skirt backwards or do a wet-exit getting into your boat, everyone sees you. Actually it's only the distance thing that stops us, we gave up being embarrassed years ago. We often launch nearby at the boat ramp or at Evening Cove and stop in during our paddle at Transfer Beach for lunch at the concession stand.

The few times that we have launched at Transfer Beach Park, we have carried our boats to the south end of the park (best beach for launching) and then paddled over to the Dunsmuir Islands and Sibell Bay (round trip of about 4 km). We have also paddled south along the shore past Holland Bank (a mud flat that sticks out quite far) to Davis Lagoon, a trip of about 7 km. There are a few interesting small coves and creeks along the way and many waterfront homes to look at. Both these paddles are good Easykayaker trips for beginners or anyone wanting a laid-back paddle.

The black sands at the north end of Transfer Beach is where coal slag was dumped years ago during this area's coal mining days. The charts refer to this area as Slag Point, but according to locals, its real name is Slack Point. Here stood the coal wharves and bunkers.

Ladysmith became an instant town when the coal-shipping terminal was built there. The owner of the Extension mine, James Dunsmuir, decided he didn't want a town at his pithead, so he ordered the buildings to be moved by the new rail line to Oyster Bay some time around 1898. By 1904, many more houses had been built and the name Oyster Bay was changed to Ladysmith. Beside the coal collieries, there was the smelter and reduction plant (where the boat basin is now located) for the Tyee Mining Company. This smelter received local copper and gold ore plus ore from as far away as Alaska.

Years later the Slack Point area became home to a large boat repair company. The boat repair company was destroyed by fire in the 1970s. You can see the remains of some concrete "waves" just inside Slack Point. Right near these old waves is the site of Ladysmith's first annual kayak paddlefest. The first paddlefest was held July 31 and August 1, 1999. Transfer Beach is now home to the Vancouver Island Paddlefest.

Our favourite paddle from Transfer Beach was a full moon paddle. On our first attempt at this, we did things very backwards. Nine of us launched and headed southeast towards Holland Banks and Davis Lagoon. As we crossed the mud flats of Holland Banks four of us decided to take advantage of the high tide and paddle up to the mouth of Holland Creek. After a wrong turn or two we found the real channel and paddled up to a large concrete culvert that leads under a wide four lane highway. The tide was high enough to paddle through the culvert and there was still some daylight left before dark. Paul and my daughter Katherine wisely turned around and headed back to join the rest of the group. Those of us who are stronger paddlers tend to take many small side excursions. The more laid-back paddlers can travel at their own speed, cover less distance, and that way the group more or less stays together.

Jan and I couldn't resist the urge and paddled into the culvert. The culvert was just wide enough to paddle in. It was longer than it looked and very dark much of the way. There was no turning around and things got spooky. I was quite relieved when it started getting lighter near the far end. The hope of finding a nice pool was quickly extinguished when I popped out into the light. Holland Creek was beautiful but the water level was low and the pool very small. I got out of my kayak on slippery sharp rocks and did a clumsy job of picking the kayak up and turning it around. The sound of a kayak bouncing on rocks is not at all musical. Jan saw what I went through and elected to back several hundred feet through the culvert in the dark. Good judgment comes from experience and much of that comes from bad judgment.

We caught up with the rest of the group in time to catch the sunset, however we were paddling in the wrong direction to really appreciate it. The moonrise was spectacular as it went from an odd shaped light on the horizon to a huge reddish ball hovering just over the water. It would be hard to find the right words to describe the beauty of its reflection on the water. Our timing was out however, because it was now time to turn around and the moon would be behind us. I did a head count three times and came up with eleven kayakers. Somewhere we had picked up two extra. On the trip back, the group occasionally stopped, turned around, and gazed at the moon.

Twenty-eight days later found eighteen of us heading out from Transfer Beach to enjoy the experience again. This time we paddled up towards the head of the harbour enjoying the sunset as we went. We had timed our departure such that we would be turning around to head back just as the moon was rising. We enjoyed the moon the whole way back to Transfer Beach.

Night paddling requires a few more safety precautions than normal day paddling. Lighting is very important. To meet Coast Guard regulations, you can buy a short, white light topped mast for kayak. The fitting mounts permanently to your kayak behind the cockpit and the mast part is removable. We use flashing bicycle lights mounted on the front and rear of our PFDs. We also have a waterproof cone shaped, flashlight type, bow light plus we carry hand held flashlights to shine at any approaching boaters. For fun we sometimes add glow sticks to our kayak decks under the bungee cords. Ideally, at night you should avoid paddling near boat traffic areas.

Another night hazard is hitting a floating log as my daughter found out. She didn't notice the large log floating low in the water until she rode up on top of it. She tried backing off it to no avail. It made her boat feel very unstable and required another kayaker to get her free of the log. For this and many other reasons people paddling at night should stay in groups.

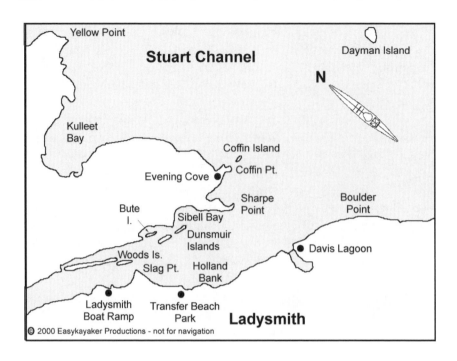

Chart #3443
Tidal Reference: Fulford Harbour

Bald Eagle in Ladysmith Harbour area

Ladysmith boat ramp

The Ladysmith boat launch is easily reached. There is a traffic light at the north end of Ladysmith where First Avenue and Ludlow Road intersect the highway. Turn onto Ludlow Road, veer right at the yield sign and go straight after the stop sign. You will soon come to the boat launch which is next to the Government Wharf. We usually launch from the gravel beach adjacent to the boat ramp. Parking is plentiful and easy.

Ladysmith Harbour and its resident islands offer a lot of casual, laid-back paddling. We have kayaked in the harbour many times exploring the coves, rocky shorelines, skirting around the islands, and dipping under the walkways and around the docks. The area is quite sheltered and the harbour is a good place to paddle when weather conditions are too iffy for more exposed areas and crossings.

Ladysmith Harbour is reasonably well protected from winds. Gary and I, and our respective families and friends, often use the harbour for quick outings. Occasionally, the wind blows the length of the harbour. Once you're across the channel you can paddle the insides of the Woods and Dunsmuir Islands. This is a nice easy kayak on its own. If you want a longer paddle, you can head southeast to Evening Cove and Coffin Point. Another nice paddle is to explore northwest to the head of the harbour. It's farther than it looks! A high tide is needed to explore all the flats and the mouths of the creeks. You can see the remains of pilings from the old Island Highway that crossed the harbour.

February had been a disastrous month of rain and cold weather. It was the first month in two years that we had not gone for a paddle. Finally, good weather arrived on a day we were free to paddle. The first Saturday in March opened up into a clear, sunny day. We felt lucky and grateful to receive a few hours of sunshine on our winter-bleached skins and rain-drenched souls.

I was paddling a Storm kayak and wearing a nylon spray skirt. While I would eventually buy a lighter, fibreglass boat, the Storm has treated me well in calm and rough weather. However, today I would slave to stretch the skirt over the lips of the cockpit. The coaming on a polymer rotomolded (plastic) boat doesn't have as sharp an edge as the coaming of a fibreglass boat. The coaming around my cockpit combined with the fact that nylon spray skirts are prone to shrinkage, left me with a sprayskirt that didn't want to fit. Everyone patiently waited for me while I slowly drifted under the dock trying to slip my skirt on. Finally, after knocking a few barnacles off with my rudder I asked Teesh to hold the back while I stretched the cover over the front lip. I smiled like the experienced kayaker that I am and said, "Thank you." I would like our readers to know that I can get my sprayskirt on quite quickly in rough weather. But if you had watched me this day and decided that you wouldn't want me to be your kayak outfitter, I would certainly understand.

As we scooted under the Government Wharf main dock and alongside one of the boat docks we heard a cheerful hello from Snuffy, a fisherman, and local Yellow Point resident. Snuffy and a crew of men were building new docks as part of a government work program. Many fishermen are working on provincial grants to give them work and new skills.

Snuffy pointed to the dock on the far side of the marina that the crew had just constructed and offered to show us his work. He hopped in a small runabout a fellow worker was in and they scooted over 2 or 3 docks, with us kayaking alongside. Snuffy described how the docks (floats) were constructed and then how they floated them off the beach. Changing the subject slightly, I asked Snuffy if he had been herring fishing. He replied, "I hate herring fishing. Take your worst job and multiply that times 10 and that's herring fishing. You work for hours on end for days, you constantly stink and you come back exhausted." I didn't ask any more questions, but his reply gave everyone a smile.

As there was a light breeze, we headed across Ladysmith Harbour toward Woods Island. The islands would protect us from the wind. It would also allow us to go up Burleith Arm (the body of water on the other side of the islands) with the wind as it's no fun to go against the wind in this long narrow channel. This is the only area in the harbour that we think much about the wind. It never gets rough on Burleith Arm but the wind can be quite focused in the 2 km stretch behind the islands.

The late winter sun warmed our hands and upper bodies. We headed southeast along Woods Island. We paddled quite close to its western rocky shoreline.

Woods and Dunsmuir Islands are unique in many ways. The sandstone shorelines are water-etched and storm-washed. A number of small caves and spaces between the inter-tidal rocks offer wonderful hiding places for raccoons, shoreline birds, and river otters. Stonecrop plants occupy the cliff edges and the occasional small, isolated rock pocket in the spray zone of the beach. This white and pink succulent plant with its distinctive yellow flower is common to Vancouver Island's east coast. Large arbutus trees, Garry oaks, cedars, firs, and the occasional maple tree cover the islands along with juniper, salal, and other flora. Along one stretch of the smaller Woods Island, kinnickinick draped over a ledge along the barren sandstone face.

Today's paddle was slow and thoughtful. With no real agenda or destination our boats meandered slowly to the southeast end of the smaller Woods Island. We decided to paddle just for the joy of it and not to go anywhere in particular. As we turned around the point we noticed a number of Goldeneye and Buffle-head ducks bobbing in the waters near shore. Alerted, perhaps by our kayaks, a group of the ducks fled the area. On the larger Woods Island a Bald Eagle was perched on a thick, dead branch of a snag. The majestic bird swept down in front of us from the lifeless tree in a swift descent toward the last fleeing duck. The duck flapped frantically just above the sea. It was still in take off mode and had not yet gained its usual flying speed. The eagle halved the distance in less than 1 or 2 seconds—the duck's fate seemed certain. We expected to see a puff of feathers as the two collided. At the very last moment the bird of prey braked with its wing tip feathers and it swept in a slow arc up until almost vertical. The ducks were soon gone. Afterwards, we speculated on the eagle's change of heart. Gary thought that the eagle was simply playing with the duck. Teesh thought that our presence caused the eagle to abort its kill.

The Bald Eagle has been quite successful on Vancouver Island's east coast. We almost always see at least one every time we go for a paddle. Its greatest enemies are habitat loss and people (just recently, 94 eagles were killed in the Duncan area by a poacher). Eagles have a sufficient wingspan to electrocute themselves on hydro lines. Last year I found an eagle in the Nanoose area with a bullet hole through its wing. Unfortunately, eagles are often poisoned too. They are on the top of their food chain and can fall prey to a poisoned environment.

Bald Eagles sometimes maintain two nests, one larger more frequented nest, and one smaller nest. The largest nests on record would be capable of holding a small car in them and weigh several tons. The white head on an eagle is a sign of maturity. They usually gain this colour in their third or fourth year of life. In my readings the only bird that the Bald Eagle gives a wide berth to is the Great Horned Owl. (Though once when I was surveying in the Pemberton area on the Lilloet River, I scared a Golden Eagle off its catch. It was sitting on a back road. The eagle's feathers literally touched both sides of the road as it took flight. Curiously, I investigated the catch and found it to be a Great Horned Owl with its neck ripped open.)

The Bald Eagle has remarkable eyesight. Apparently, it can see a rabbit clearly (to the eagle it looks the size of a goat) from a kilometre high and has twice as many colour cones in its eyes as a human.

We stopped paddling shortly after the eagle display and rafted the boats together for a cookie break. We drifted past a houseboat called the Watership Down, a stern mounted paddlewheeler that was underway toward town and then by some log booms of yellow cedar. Several boomboats were anchored at a private log sorting dock on our right. While rafted up, the light wind sailed us as a group of 4 kayaks (paddles sitting across each other's cockpits) northwest up Burleith Arm. After eating our cream-filled delights we paddled to the tip of the larger Woods Island. We had checked the tide tables before launching as we always do. On a tide of three feet or lower, a short portage is required to round this tip of the island. Today there was lots of depth and just a few rocks to maneuver around. Just around the point is Page Point Inn, a favourite waterfront eating establishment, marina and bed & breakfast. We paddled around the small set of docks looking at the various boats and then headed southeast along Woods Island again.

After a short distance we turned and headed toward the Ladysmith boat ramp. Just before the boat ramp we crossed over to the Ladysmith shore and cruised by the log booms in front of Domans mills looking for seals. Sometimes later in the year we will see moms with their pups hauled out on the logs there.

First Seaward kayak built in Ladysmith
on a paddle in Ladysmith Harbour

View of Dunsmuir Islands from the Ladysmith
Amphitheatre

Low tide at Evening Cove

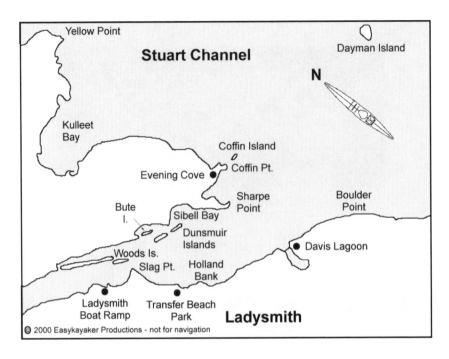

Chart #3443
Tidal Reference: Fulford Harbour

Katherine's first paddle, age 9, destination Evening Cove

Evening Cove—North Oyster

Evening Cove is a nice place to visit even if you aren't kayaking. If you're coming from the Ladysmith direction on the highway, continue north of Ladysmith, pass the Mohawk gas station at the old Ivy Green and turn right onto Brenton-Page Road. If you're coming from the Nanaimo direction on the highway, travel south past the Nanaimo Airport, past the lights at Cedar Road and then turn left onto Brenton-Page Road. The turnoff is well marked plus there's a sign for Page Point Inn.

Brenton-Page Road is named after John Brenton and David Page, who homesteaded here in the early 1870s. The waterfront portion of David Page's homestead is made up of smaller properties including the land that Mañana Lodge and Marina (now Page Point Inn) occupies. My wife, daughter and I own and live on the remainder of David Page's property, which is now BC Managed Forest 127. We practice small-scale forestry in what we feel is an environmentally responsible manner.

The road name changes from Brenton-Page Road to Shell Beach Road and then again to Evening Cove Road. You won't likely notice the changed name until you drive along the road. Even the locals get confused as to where the names actually change. About 100 feet (30 metres) from the road's end, turn right onto Elliott Way. The beach and launch site is at the end of Elliott Way and is named Elliott Park.

It was January 2nd and a beautiful clear sunny winter day. Paula had phoned about 8:30 A.M. from Victoria, wanting to take me up on that offer to go paddling. Tony was thinking about buying a kayak and they wanted to try ours out. Paula and Tony planned to each buy a kayak eventually. Last summer they paddled our double with us. After that paddle, they commented that two singles would be more fun. Most people seem to prefer singles to doubles.

Last time they were out we launched at the Ladysmith Boat Ramp and paddled around Woods Islands and the Page Point Inn area. With a two-hour drive for them, I wanted to launch from somewhere nearby. Also, it was January 2nd and weather conditions could change quickly. We settled on Evening Cove, a regional park located between Ladysmith and Yellow Point. This is my favourite and most often used launch site. It has a nice beach, warm water for swimming in the summer and is seldom crowded. Access is good, but a gate means the boats and gear have to be carried a short distance. Fortunately, there's little elevation change down to the beach and the trail is easy.

Usually one of us will grab two bows and the other two sterns. In this fashion we can carry two boats full of gear down to the beach at once. The sterns are heaviest so bows are the favourite of many. For day trips, I load my food and extras in the front hatch to try and balance the load for carrying. Most of the trail at Evening Cove is two boats wide.

Paula, Tony and their three-year old daughter, Numa arrived around 11 A.M. My daughter (under my wife's supervision) got a chance to try out babysitting for the first time. I had the PFDs, sprayskirts, paddles, safety gear and lunch already loaded. They didn't have sunglasses, so we did a quick search for some spares. I'm a firm believer in wearing a cap with a brim and sunglasses when kayaking on a sunny day. We also try to plan our route so we won't be going directly into the sun, as the reflection off the water can be blinding.

Fifteen minutes later we were at the beach and in another fifteen minutes we were paddling. When just Paul and I go out, we are a finely polished team, usually in the water within a few minutes of parking. With very few words spoken, each of us works efficiently ~ untying the boats, loading gear and packing it all down to the water.

Paula had never paddled a single before, but Tony is a kayaker from way back, although most of his experience is with white water (river) kayaking. Most ocean going kayakers paddle with their blades parallel while white water kayakers keep their blades feathered at 90 degrees. There is a significant reason for this difference. In ocean touring having both blades parallel allows for quick bracing and is also gentler on your wrists. The opposed white water blades are to make sure that the turned blade will cut through the water if it hits a wave. I have accidentally hit water with my forwarding moving paddle blade and can see the sense in this paddling style. Once you learn to paddle one way, most people don't change and sure enough, Tony assembled his paddle in the white water fashion.

Evening Cove offers a few choices of where to paddle. We have launched from here to go to Kulleet Bay, Yellow Point, Thetis and other Gulf Islands and many trips into Ladysmith Harbour. When launching Ladysmith Harbour is to the right, Coffin Point is to the left, and just past that is a very small island with a light named Coffin Island. Until recently the home tucked in behind Coffin Point belonged to Mr. Elliott. He is of First Nations descent and his family has lived here for very many years.

According to Mr. Elliott the name comes from the practice before the coming of white man of placing the dead in cedar boxes and leaving them on the island. He told me that although the higher-ranking Natives were buried, the normal custom was not to bury the dead, but to place them in boxes at the base of bluffs and on islands. Many of these dead have now been buried in the First Nations cemetery, but Mr. Elliott feels some grave sites probably still exist on his Coffin Point property. Please treat this area with respect if you stop here.

Paula, Tony and I paddled around Coffin Point and were hit by a light but very cold wind. We tucked into the shallow bay just north of Coffin Point and skimmed over some large oyster racks that are part of an oyster lease. Once north of the oyster lease, this is all First Nations land. I thought back to the very foggy late winter day a year ago that Paul and I continued along north to Kulleet Bay. The fog had covered everything above the 20-foot elevation level, which made things a bit surrealistic. Two river otters had been playing and seemed to be going our way. We traveled with the otters for about half an hour. They seemed to be having so much fun frolicking with each other.

Today Paula, Tony and I turned out into Stuart Channel and felt the cold wind. We paddled toward Thetis Island for a couple of minutes. A few hot summer days have found me paddling over to Thetis with friends to swim and picnic along the deserted northwestern shoreline. As much as I dislike the boredom of the 4 km (each way) crossing, it's worth it when you get there. Once Paula, Tony and I got a short distance from shore, we rode the waves and wind over to Coffin Island, paddled around the island and into the mouth of Ladysmith Harbour. We could see our launch site as we paddled by. We were about half a kilometre from shore and were taking full advantage of what wave action there was to push us toward Sharpe Point.

It had been quite rough around Coffin Island, but the harbour was almost flat calm by the time we got to Sharpe Point. I was able to shout "Hi" to Ron as we paddled by his and Terry's new home on the point. We then paddled around the two Dunsmuir Islands. There is an incredible Native shellfish midden inside the western Dunsmuir Island that has almost caused me to run aground at high and medium tides. At low tide the midden is exposed and you can see how extensive it is.

Between the two islands is a reef and islet. At a low tide this sandy white beach, made up entirely of crushed shells, is a very easy place to land your kayak. It's also a great spot for a picnic lunch. You can walk to both islands. Landing can be a challenge at a high tide.

I thought back to an evening, last summer. Instead of going to Transfer Beach to watch Ladysmith's Dogwood Days (BC Day) fireworks, Paul,

Imelda, their son, Jordan and I paddled out to this islet to watch the fireworks. My wife and daughter were away visiting family in Saskatoon at the time.

The tide was high the evening Paul's family and I had come out to watch the fireworks. We did find a place to land (one kayak at a time), but footing was poor for getting out of the boats. According to the tide table, the tide wouldn't change much over the next few hours so we hauled the boats out of the water and made ourselves comfortable on the islet to wait for dark and the fireworks.

As soon as we sat down an otter popped up in the water about 20 feet in front of us. It took a good long look at us and then submerged. A moment later it popped up again a bit to the left and sat there like a dog begging with its front paws in the air. As soon as it disappeared, a young raccoon swam over from the nearby island and walked up to us. It stopped about six feet away and looked at us. Usually we view wildlife, but tonight it seemed that wildlife was viewing us. The raccoon went over and checked out all the kayaks one by one. He swam back to his island and then came back to sit with us for about half an hour until the fireworks started.

Paddling back in the dark was quite an experience. It was our first, intentional nighttime paddle. We had lights and glow sticks on the boats, plus hand held flashlights on deck to shine at any approaching traffic. It was so dark that we couldn't see the wakes from boats leaving the harbour until the wakes hit us. We could make out the shore but not submerged rocks or reefs. Fortunately, we knew this coast very well and were able to stay close enough to shore to avoid boat traffic, but far enough out to avoid scraping our bottoms. We got a chuckle listening to the comments of some campers on one of the beaches, who were trying to figure out what we were. They could see our lights close to the water and our quietness combined with our speed had them mystified for a minute or two.

Today, as Paula, Tony and I paddled around the Dunsmuirs, the tide was too high to land easily, so we continued over to and around Bute Island and started heading back, which took us into Sibell Bay and by the Shell Beach First Nations community. Half way between Sibell Bay and Sharpe Point we pulled into the abandoned mystified campers' campsite for a lunch stop.

The beach along here is more pebbly than sandy, but there are lots of shells to make beachcombing enjoyable. One of our kids' games is to find a hunk of driftwood, toss it about 15 feet from shore, then sit down and take turns tossing pebbles at it. It's amazing how bad our aim is some days.

After lunch we paddled into the cove that is the real Evening Cove (a little southwest of the launch site) and explored every nook and cranny that the tide allowed us to access. When we got back to the launch site, Paula and I packed two boats to the trailer while Tony tried out the boat Paula had been paddling.

Back home I made a round of Northern Lights to warm us up. My recipe is hot chocolate, coffee liqueur, orange brandy and a scoop or two of vanilla ice cream. I tried this recipe one evening in the Broken Islands, but substituted sweetened condensed milk for the ice cream. It was too sweet and hard to clean the cups after because of the canned condensed milk. One of our fellow campers had a tall cup, which he left to clean in the morning light. Come morning we found his cup had a very sticky mouse trapped in it. We let the mouse loose and boiled the cup clean. I'll try evaporated milk next time we're camping.

Dunsmuir Island in Ladysmith Harbour

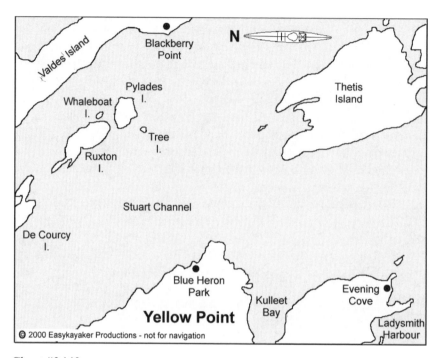

Chart #3443
Tidal Reference: Fulford Harbour

Blue Heron photo
by Jan Pullinger

Blue Heron Park—Yellow Point

Cedar is the community just south of Nanaimo. Yellow Point is south of Cedar and north of Ladysmith. The main road through Cedar is Cedar Road, a U-shaped road, accessible from the Island Highway in two places. Yellow Point Road, another U-shaped road, passes through Yellow Point. It's accessible from Cedar Rd. in two locations. The entrance to Blue Heron Park is a very short road off Yellow Point Road called Westby Road. It's located just north of Yellow Point Lodge. Westby Road was named after Arnold Westby, who was a local farmer and pioneer hatchery operator, and was instrumental in the creation of Blue Heron Park.

It had been about a month since we last paddled. With everyone's work schedules and short daylight hours, only weekends and holidays were available for kayaking. The last four weekends had either been monsoon rains and gale force winds, or they were taken up with family obligations and community work parties. We had e-mailed back and forth about going paddling on Saturday, December 5th but things got in the way so we decided Sunday would be the day. That is, of course, weather permitting.

It's hard to predict good weather in early December. The last few weeks it had rained almost daily (at least it seemed that way). Early Saturday brought more rain and strong gusts of wind (40 km/hr). Sunday proved to be a better day.

On Sunday morning I awoke late. My wife and I had attended the company Christmas party and we had stayed up later than usual. While lying in bed I could see a blue sky and still trees. I rolled over and switched on the Coast Guard weather channel—60% chance of rain. The clear skies convinced me otherwise. After listening to the full synopsis, the day would deteriorate into rain and winds by late afternoon. Well that was then and this is now I thought.

Paul phoned while I was listening to the 9 A.M. news on CBC radio. We agreed to launch at Blue Heron Park. He would come over and help me load boats and gear in about an hour. Blue Heron Park is an easy launch site. Other than a boat ramp, it's probably one of the easiest local sites to quickly and safely launch your boat.

Once the CBC news broadcast was over, I dragged myself from bed and gazed at the frosty field outside the window. Blue sky or not, my long underwear beckoned me. I made some breakfast, kissed my wife and daughter goodbye, as they headed for church. I started getting gear and a paddling snack together.

Paul showed up right on time. We loaded the boats and gear. On the way we stopped off at the Chuckwagon market to pick up some extra kayaking snacks. This has become a ritual for most of the paddling we do. It may not be the Chuckwagon, but usually we stop at some store. A few minutes later we headed into the deserted parking lot of Blue Heron Park.

Blue Heron is a North Oyster Community Park. It even has a porta-pottie type outhouse facility, which is something most launch sites don't have. From the parking lot there is a short, wide, trail to the water. The sandstone, gently sloped walk to the water's edge can vary from a few feet to several hundred feet depending on the tide. A very high tide of 11.5 feet an hour earlier meant a short walk for us.

With it being only a few degrees above freezing, we weren't looking forward to getting our feet wet. Paul and I both wear neoprene diving boots for kayaking, but they don't usually keep our feet dry. I was quite surprised to see Paul sit down on a log just before launching with his thermos. In all the paddling we've done, we have seldom taken hot drinks along and usually we are in a hurry to get into the boats. I thought, "Does Paul really need that hot drink?" Before I could say anything, Paul told me that he was going to try an old diver's trick of pouring hot water into his boots to keep his feet warm. We now wear waterproof paddling socks which actually do keep our feet dry.

When launching at Blue Heron Park there are a lot of options for paddling. You can go left (northwest) toward Boat Harbour or you can go right (southeast) toward Yellow Point Lodge and Ladysmith. Another option is to head straight out and cross to Pylades and Ruxton Islands (4.5 km) or head southeast to Thetis Island (4 km). We really weren't in the mood to do a long, boring crossing on a cold day with the threat of approaching, bad weather. A couple of years ago, we had launched at Blue Heron Park and paddled to Thetis Island. After a great paddle we walked onto the ferry carrying our kayaks. The ferry took us to Chemainus where my wife picked us up. Another time with another paddling partner on a warm beautiful day, I paddled to Thetis Island, circumnavigated it and returned back to nearby Evening Cove (a long paddle for me). For those who like long crossings, once across to Pylades Island you can island hop north to camp at De Courcy Island's Pirates Cove Park or west to camp on Valdes Island's Blackberry Point. (We prefer other routes to get to both destinations and cover them in other sections along with details of the campsites and routes.)

Today we decided to go to the left and head up the coast exploring all the little coves. We wouldn't be paddling into the sun! As we launched I managed to get my boat in the water barely wetting my feet. It was not a graceful maneuver but the boat didn't rub bottom. A change of water colour approximately 200 feet offshore showed the telltale signs of wind. We soon glided across a glassy surface into a slightly ruffled water with a barely noticeable wind.

Abundant bird life surrounded us. A Bald Eagle cried as it flew over us and landed in a nearby tree. Groups of small black and white duck-like birds swam nearby and seemed unafraid of us. A cormorant sat on a mooring buoy. A small loon or grebe swam past. A very nervous bird on a mooring buoy rocked back and forth trying to decide whether or not to fly away. It was the colour of a Great Blue Heron but looked like a large cormorant. I thought that it was a Great Blue Heron, but just then it took off and flew like a cormorant. Paul remarked that a lot of these birds weren't here in the summer. Later at home I got out my bird book and looked some of them up. The black and white ducks turned out to be Buffleheads which, according to the book, summer on wooded lakes and rivers and winter in tidewater. I never did identify the Great Blue Cormorant type bird.

Paddling along was great. A slight wind came up and helped us along. The currents in this area are very minor (1 knot). They flood north and ebb south. We were on an ebb tide going against it but didn't feel it at all. The high tide allowed us to explore many coves and small inlets along the shore. We missed the wealth of shells, white beaches and washed up objects that come with paddling and beachcombing this area at low tide.

We reached Roberts Memorial Provincial Park at noon and decided to have a snack. Roberts Park is only a 2.5 km paddle from Blue Heron Park and easily recognized by a six-foot high chainlink fence extending out to the high tide line. There is a sign on the fence that reads "Provincial Park Boundary." I was still full from last night's Christmas Party dinner and it was chilly on shore (getting out I didn't manage to keep dry feet). On a warmer day it would have been nice to walk some of the 0.5 km wooded trail that runs from Yellow Point Road to the beach at Roberts Park.

We had planned to travel further up the coast, but the wind (which would be against us on the way back) was picking up and clouds were appearing. We decided to head back in case the weather turned. Paul put more warm water in his boots and I managed to get more cold water in mine getting back into the boat. By staying close to shore we avoided the increasing wind. We were surprised at how much of this area was undeveloped and were impressed by the few houses that we did see. We only saw one boat and almost no one on shore.

We had only paddled 5 km when we got back to the launch site, so we decided to paddle around Yellow Point and view Yellow Point Lodge from the water. From there we explored some of the coves southwest of Yellow Point. About this time we started discussing the temperature of our feet. The wind waves were picking up (still quite small) and we decided it was time to head back. On the way back the sun came out to shine across the fresh snow capped mountains on the mainland. The gorgeous view, we knew, captured the essence of our short kayak trip.

Landing back at Blue Heron Park, we saw an artist with an easel painting the same view. Along the beach, a woman walked two very happy dogs. We got our gear to the parking lot and started getting dry socks and shoes on. About this time I had a nice conversation with a fellow who looked to be in his 80s. He had just come from hiking with his wife in Yellow Point Park, but it was such a nice day that he wanted to enjoy the outdoors a little more before going home.

It was a lazy and easy paddle, only about 8 km, but very enjoyable and relaxing. All 8 km had been "rudder up" type paddling, our favourite type of kayaking. The highlight of the day for me was coming out of a shady, long, narrow inlet and catching the view of a silhouetted gull on a low rock with sunny waterways and distant islands behind. I thought that it would make a wonderful picture if I had a camera, however I knew that such a view could never be captured anywhere but in the mind's eye.

Footnote from Paul:

It was a truly, relaxing day for me except for one incident. I discovered that my steel thermos kept the boiling water a little too hot. I gladly poured hot water into them and pulled on a boot. What a mistake! After a short, muffled scream the boot quickly came off. Next trip and tip—don't boil the water but put it in hot!

Footnote from Gary:

During the paddle we talked about some of the major trips that we would like to do this coming summer. When we got back home and stowed our boats and gear away, we sat down to look at the newest chart I had bought. With a Northern Lights in hand (hot chocolate, orange brandy, coffee liquer and a scoop of vanilla ice cream) we studied the chart for Kyuquot Sound and Rugged Point Marine Provincial Park. I went and got my copy of Michael Blades' book *Day of Two Sunsets* (Chapter Two—Kapoose) and read his account of paddling this area. Paul left after that to go home and shovel manure out of the horse barn and I went out to string Christmas lights. About 7 P.M. the wind and rain arrived. The next morning the wind gusted to 90 km/hr and some of the BC Ferry sailings were canceled.

Many eyes may watch you paddle by
Photo by Jan Pullinger

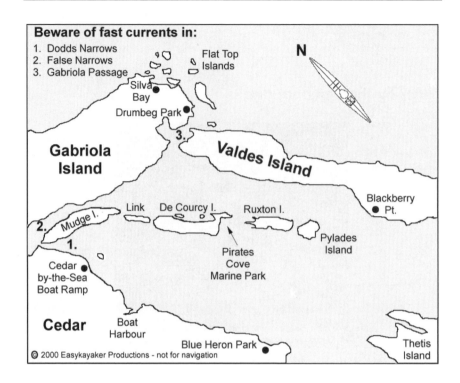

Chart #3443
Tidal Reference: Fulford Harbour

Valdes Island

Cedar-by-the-Sea boat ramp

To access this launch, turn off the Island Highway onto Cedar Road, turn onto MacMillan Road, then onto Holden-Corso Road, Barnes Road, Murdock Road, and finally, left onto Nelson Road. If that sounds confusing, it might be a wise idea to have an area map with you. The boat ramp is at the bottom of Nelson Road.

One of my first clear memories of soft adventure kayaking was an evening paddle along the shoreline from the Cedar-by-the-Sea boat ramp south to Blue Heron Park. We were trying out a Necky Amaruk double kayak that Gary had recently purchased. We left my car at Blue Heron Park and drove to our launch site in Gary's car. This allowed us to make that paddle a one-way trip. The nice thing about one way trips is that you can go with the wind and current the whole way. With all the jogs to explore interesting coves and inlets, our trip scaled at about 9 km on the chart. We expected the paddle to take a little over two hours. With help from the wind and tidal currents, we were quite surprised to arrive at Blue Heron after only 90 minutes.

Since then, we have paddled many times from the Cedar-by-the-Sea boat ramp, sometimes to Boat Harbour and back, but mostly over to Link Island and the De Courcy Group. There's nothing more soothing than a quiet paddle along a rocky shoreline as the sunlight dances through the branches and leaves of the coastal arbutus and fir trees. The afternoon winds have usually died, the water is still and crystal clear, and the day seems to be coming to a rest. An evening paddle from Cedar-by-the-Sea to Blue Heron is the zen of paddling when winds are calm.

The Cedar-by-the-Sea boat ramp is very popular on long weekends and holidays. Local boaters quickly fill the small parking area and line the streets. It's one of the busier launches in the Nanaimo area. However, don't let that deter you from frolicking in nearby waters! There are many kayaking trips from this vantage launch site, so many in fact that kayak launchings here now outnumber motorboat launchings.

Today's trip was going to take us to De Courcy Island's Pirate's Cove

Marine Park and back. It was a beautiful calm spring day, a perfect day to get our winter-kayaking arms in shape for the longer summer trips to come. I'm sure we were releasing the week's work tension and taking it out on the tensile strength of our paddles.

A few minutes after we slid our kayaks into the waters of Stuart Channel, we were cruising past the seals on the islets and reefs just south of Round Island. We went well around the wildlife rather than taking the shortcut between Round Island and the islets. As Dodd Narrows is not far away, mild eddies are often present on the south and east sides of Round Island, however we didn't notice any today.

The crossing to the south end of Link Island from Round Island took about 40 minutes. We felt the tug from the flooding tide toward Dodd's Narrows but it didn't really slow us down (the chart reads 3 knots of tidal current but this is only at maximum tides). I wouldn't hesitate to take my family on this crossing.

We reached Link Island and followed its shoreline south to the 'Hole in the Wall', a narrow passage, between Link and De Courcy Island. You can cross between Mudge and Link Island but you will have to portage across a wide shell beach called a tombolo. Today we decided to paddle through the 'Hole in the Wall', along the east coast of De Courcy, turn into Ruxton Passage, paddle back up the west coast of De Courcy and then head back to Cedar-by-the-Sea.

'Hole in the Wall' is not passable at low tide and, from experience, I would not recommend portaging it as the rocks are slippery and the holes between are deep. Fortunately the tide was high enough for us to wind our way between the rocks and into the unnamed bay between the two islands. The house to our right was something to behold and so were the boats and floatplane moored there. On the north shore we heard two raccoons fighting, what wild sounds!

Ideally one should go south along De Courcy during an ebb tide and north during a flood tide. We would be doing the opposite, but the tidal change was minimal today, so it really didn't matter much.

On our way south we saw a doe and her spotted fawn grazing on the edge of a low bluff. Gary took a picture of them as we paddled by. Fortunately both deer and raccoons are not overly shy of kayaks quietly gliding by. We usually see one or the other on our paddles along De Courcy Island.

The east side of De Courcy has some nice little islands to paddle along and some pretty nice homes. A large bay named Pirates Cove at the south end of the east side is a favourite for motorboaters that come to this Provincial Marine Park. Kayakers and canoeists normally use the landing on the other side, off Ruxton Passage.

As it was still the shoulder season, there weren't many people at Pirate's Cove. In the summer it can be quite a zoo. Camping here is always a raccoon event. If you sleep outside without a tent, you will likely be walked on by a raccoon some time during the night.

On the occasional year during spring, Pirate's Cove can have an awful lot of mosquitoes, but most years they aren't a problem as was the case today. There is also some Poison Oak growing here. This plant is very rare (fortunately) in British Columbia and so it's considered special. To the best of our knowledge, De Courcy Island is the only large Gulf Island where you have to be careful to avoid coming in contact with Poison Oak.

We had a nice lunch at the park. Few of our lunch sites come complete with fresh water, picnic tables and outhouses such as this site has. After lunch we paddled the rest of Ruxton Passage and then headed back up along the wonderful cliffs and rock formations of the west side of De Courcy Island. Just before Link Island, we turned homeward and started our return crossing of Stuart Channel. The water had a rolling mirror effect that was so incredibly beautiful it was almost mesmerizing.

All too soon our Easykayaker paddle was over—we had kayaked about 15 km. On the way home we stopped at the Crow & Gate Pub for a beer and to talk about future overnight trips from Cedar-by-the-Sea to Blackberry Point on Valdes Island. We also discussed using this launch to paddle through Dodd Narrows, False Narrows and Gabriola Passage, trips only recommended for experienced paddlers and even then only at slack tides or during a minor tide change.

Gary off Valdes Island rock formations

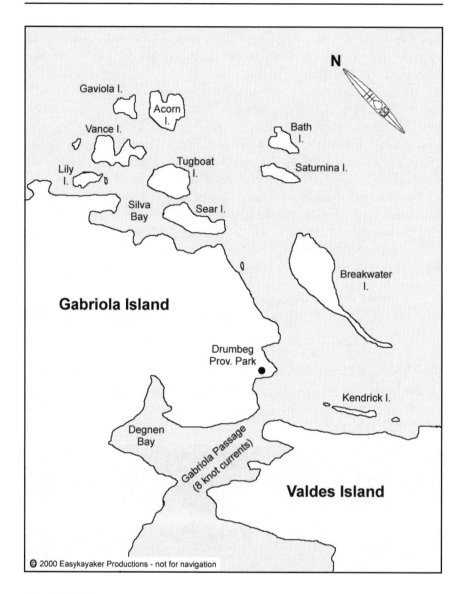

Chart #3443
Tidal Reference: Point Atkinson

Paddling the Gabriola Flat Tops

The Gabriola Island ferry departs from downtown Nanaimo's waterfront. Once on Gabriola, follow South Road and then Stalker Road to Drumbeg Provincial Park. Be careful when launching not to stray too close to the fast moving waters of Gabriola Passage.

I've flown over the Flat Tops many times and have frequently sailed by aboard the BC Ferries Duke Point to Tsawwassen run. Most of those times I would rather have been kayaking the Flat Tops instead of heading for the mainland. They say that there's always time for what you make time for. So one late spring day we made time to paddle the Flat Tops.

This first day paddle into Gabriola's Flat Top Islands was wonderful. I had recently purchased my first fibreglass kayak, a Current Designs Solstice, and today was to be its maiden voyage. Until now I'd been paddling a plastic Necky Narpa and a wooden Cape Charles.

Paul, Jan, Dale and I trailered the four kayaks into Nanaimo and onto the Gabriola ferry. As we sat on the ferry we watched the whitecapping seas and we were a little apprehensive of the water conditions we might encounter further out in the Straits later that day. After disembarking from the ferry, we drove across Gabriola to Silva Bay at the far end of the island (east end of Gabriola). We weren't sure exactly where to launch from, but finally decided to launch at the old boat ways near the marinas and we were soon in the protected bay surrounded by six of the eleven Flat Top Islands.

It was a sunny May day, the winds were much weaker than on the Nanaimo side of Gabriola and they were blowing from the northwest. We decided to use the shelter of the islands and head to Lily Island, the northernmost island, and then paddle outside into the Strait of Georgia to see what the sea conditions were like. We were quite surprised by how calm it was and we headed further out to watch a freighter go by. Our game plan was to paddle around and outside each island using the wind to push us south. As Easykayakers we often designed our day's paddle with 'ease of paddle' in mind.

We were still on the outside of Gaviola Island (a small island north of Gabriola Island), but just heading into a channel between Gaviola and Acorn Island when the wake from the freighter struck us. It couldn't have been more perfect. The wave speed, size, direction and shape made surfing easy and fast.

We managed to visit every island except the two southern ones, Breakwater and Kendrick Islands. The sandbar and beautiful beach between Bath and Saturnina Islands was an ideal place for lunch and a rest. After lunch we visited two more islands before heading back to Silva Bay. The tide was low when we reached Silva Bay and the mud made landing very interesting. We looked the area over carefully and then chose our spot to get muddy. It looked worse than it really was, as the mud was quite firm.

Our next trip to this area found Jan, Dale and myself launching at Degnen Bay and paddling through Gabriola Passage near slack tide one early October day. This is not an Easykayaker recommended route as the currents can reach 8 or 9 knots! Slack current varies time-wise from slack tide here. Today the variation was approximately 2 ½ hours. Even at slack water the trip was interesting through Gabriola Passage as we crossed diagonally from Gabriola to Valdes Island. We hit intermittent streams of water heading both directions but nothing very strong. In theory the current was still flooding so we went between Kendrick Island and Valdes Island hoping for a free ride.

With a slightly stronger northwest wind than our first trip we quickly got bored with Valdes's east coast and headed toward Breakwater Island. Part way up the east side of Breakwater we pulled onto the beach for a snack just across from the navigational light on the island's west side. The island is very narrow here. There must have been a 'cheaper by the hundred' sale on "No Trespassing" signs as this island is peppered with them. Back in our kayaks, we managed to hide from the wind until we got to the northern tip of Breakwater Island.

The crossing over to Sear and Tugboat Islands wasn't far, but the headwinds and a very slight current made us work for it. As soon as we hit the lee of the islands conditions improved considerably. The time was approaching to start heading home so after a short paddle exploring Silva Bay we headed out between Tugboat and Sear Islands to use the wind to carry us back. It was a good idea, but at that moment the wind decided to lessen.

We pulled into Drumberg Park and watched two otters at play on a rock. The park warranted a bit of a walk and some exploring. It appears to be a great launch site at the right tidal flows and we will use it next time we want to launch near the Flat Tops. The only concern is that it is adjacent to Gabriola Passage and currents could seriously affect paddling. Getting pulled into the passage when it's really running could be deadly. We were about to get a first hand taste of this passage at only a minor tidal flow.

The tide change was only a couple of feet between high and low tides during the time period when we were going to run the passage. The current would only be three knots or so. We pulled out of Drumberg Park and headed into the narrow part of the passage. As we approached the narrows, it looked like we were entering a fast-moving river complete with small standing waves. We sped through the narrowest point of the passage. The current was taking us away from our destination of Degnen Bay at a 45 degree angle, so we turned out of the current and headed closer to shore and into the glassy looking water of the eddies. That was a mistake. In front of me a hole in the water opened up almost the size of my boat. The whirlpool was only about 6" deep, but not something I wanted to paddle through. My paddles felt like they were going through air and not water as I tried to power-stroke away. Steering was a full time job. Just as I was skirting the edge of the whirlpool, it disappeared only for a small one to open up on my left, then another on my right. Jan called to me that we should head back into the fast water. The same thought had occurred to me. We all started back toward the fast water in order to get away from these spinning currents, but as we neared the fast moving tidal stream, our drift had taken us far enough along that the water conditions in the eddies were no longer challenging.

At this point we saw a 30' cabin cruiser attempting to go against the fast water. We were content to drift in the eddies and watch the powerboat's progress. It had lots of power but couldn't keep from being swept around 180 degrees before even getting close to the narrows. They finally gave up after several attempts and headed somewhere else. That was the most powerful 3-knot current I've ever seen! So much for 3 knots being comfortable if you are going the same way as the current. This experience is definitely not a recommended Easykayaker trip.

An interesting note to add is that the Gabriola Passage area is in the process of becoming a Marine Protected Area. It's abundant and diverse in marine life with over 230 species of algae, sponges, mollusks, sea stars, crustaceans, worms, fishes and marine mammals in the area. Don't be surprised to see divers in the Flat Top area, as it's a favourite for this activity.

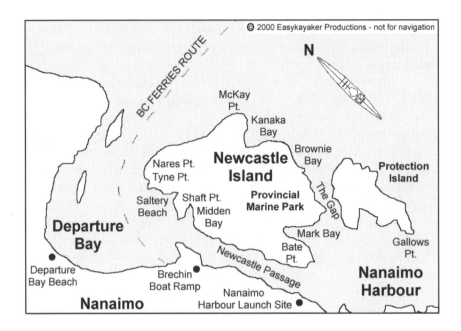

© 2000 Easykayaker Productions - not for navigation

N

BC FERRIES ROUTE

McKay Pt.

Kanaka Bay

Brownie Bay

Nares Pt.
Tyne Pt.

Newcastle Island

Protection Island

Saltery Beach

Shaft Pt.

Midden Bay

Provincial Marine Park

The Gap

Departure Bay

Departure Bay Beach

Brechin Boat Ramp

Newcastle Passage

Mark Bay

Bate Pt.

Nanaimo Harbour Launch Site

Nanaimo

Nanaimo Harbour

Gallows Pt.

Chart #3443
Tidal Reference: Point Atkinson

Nanaimo Harbour

Just south of the Nanaimo Yacht Club is a great little launch site by a sign for the Queen Elizabeth II Promenade. The launch site and the promenade entrance are located in Nanaimo on Newcastle Avenue near Benson Street. There is usually free parking close by and the distance that the boats need to be carried is short and not very steep.

The launch area is a very small sandy cove that holds only a few kayaks at high tide, but is much larger at low tide. This site is probably the best kayak access to Newcastle Island Passage, Newcastle Island, Protection Island and Nanaimo Harbour.

In July when my wife and daughter were on holiday in Saskatoon I received an invite from Rob and his wife Jackie for supper. Rob had been out on his first paddle with Paul and myself in the Chemainus area a couple weeks before. Today I suggested to Rob that we go for a paddle before supper. I wanted to look at a kevlar kayak for sale on Protection Island. I picked up Rob at his home in Nanaimo and we headed to the water.

We unloaded the boats at the park and then I parked the 4Runner nearby. It was a warm sunny day but there was some wind and chop. Fortunately the launch site is protected and calm. The stretch of water from Nanaimo Harbour to Newcastle Island Passage seldom becomes very rough, but can have winds to paddle against. Outside the gap past the two islands is a different story and it can be quite rough. We stowed our gear in the hatches and put on our sprayskirts and PFDs (personal floatation devices). Rob grabbed the sterns of both boats and I grabbed the bows. Down to the water we went and off we paddled.

This is a very busy area with boat and some seaplane traffic. By staying near shore you are usually safe and out of harms way. When out in open water you should keep your eyes peeled for anything bigger than your craft. About 30 seconds after launching you're at the south end of Newcastle Island Passage. If it's a windy day and you're planning to go around Newcastle Island, I would recommend paddling through Newcastle Island Passage against the wind. That way you will be with the wind on the outside of Newcastle Island (see the section on the Brechin boat launch for details on circumnavigating Newcastle Island).

Crossing the Passage took less than two minutes once there was a break in boat traffic. Once across we started following the shore of Newcastle Island heading south. Newcastle Island is a large Provincial Marine Park (about 2 ½ km long as the crow flies and 10 km in circumference as the kayak paddles). It offers camping, hiking, swimming, a museum, a seasonal cafe and a lot more.

Newcastle Island has an interesting and rich history. Several coal mines stretch under the water to both Protection and Newcastle Island. Inland, on the northeast side of the island, a huge air vent still exists. The openings of the mines can be found on the north end of the island.

Quarries exist on the Newcastle Island Passage side. The sandstone blocks were used in several famous buildings along the West Coast. Herring salteries, shipyards, and a rich First Nations history are all part of the discovery of this once luxurious Canadian Pacific Railway recreational park. Bill Merilees has recently written a book titled, *Newcastle Island – A Place of Discovery* on the history of the island (ISBN 1-895811-58-9).

Once around Bate Point we followed the shore eastward across Mark Bay. There were some beautiful boats anchored in Nanaimo Harbour. We paddled close to a few that had people out on deck and spoke briefly to them as our boats glided by. We've met some interesting people this way. Once past Mark Bay we crossed over to Protection Island and started looking for the landmarks that I was given.

I was told to look for a sailboat and rowboat moored together after a yellow house but before a brown house. This won't be easy I thought, as it seemed every house was either yellow or brown and most boats in view fit the rest of the description. However, on shore I could see a couple carrying a kayak down to the water's edge. As we got closer, I recognized the couple and knew we were in the right spot. We slipped up onto the sandy beach and got out to look at what might become my daughter's next kayak.

Besides the obvious handling and comfort performance, a boat, in my mind, needs easy access hatch covers and should to be beautiful to look at. Although this boat was light as a feather being kevlar, it lost points elsewhere. When Sandy told me that she hadn't really made up her mind about selling it, I had already decided it wasn't the boat for Katherine. Sandy insisted that I take it for a paddle, which I did. It handled very well, but after owning four kayaks and paddling many others, I had become fussy.

Rob and I decided to finish paddling "the Gap" between Newcastle and Protection Islands and see how rough it was on the outside. As Rob hadn't been to Newcastle Island before, we pulled into Brownie Bay to look at the camping area. Rob has two small children, Dalton and Sienna, and the family enjoys camping. After a brief walk, we were back in the boats.

The wind had calmed as we left the Gap, but there was still a breeze. We turned north and traveled along the outside shore on Newcastle Island and admired the view of the snow capped mainland mountains across the Strait of Georgia. After what seemed like 20 minutes we came to the large bay on the Vancouver side of the island.

It is named Kanaka Bay after a Kanaka (Hawaiian or South Pacific Island native) who axe murdered his First Nations wife, in-laws and his child in 1868. The police found him at a campfire near the beach here. He was convicted and hanged in 1869. Neither the First Nation people nor the area Kanakas would accept his body for burial. He was finally laid to rest in an unmarked grave near Kanaka Bay. Unfortunately, 30 years later his casket, which contained his skeleton and well preserved leather shoes, was accidentally dug up when a new coal mining shaft was started there. A coroner's inquest was held and the forgotten tale of Peter Kakua the axe murderer was brought to light once more. Peter was buried once again in an unmarked grave near Kanaka Bay. His ghost stalks the campgrounds on Newcastle Island nightly, or so the story around the campfire goes.

We came into the southern entrance of the bay. At low tide this entrance is dry. After beaching the boats, we walked along the shore to the northern tip of the bay. Actually we waded most of the way as the water was clear and the marine life was fantastic. It was warm enough for a swim, but we were content just to wade.

Back in our boats, we paddled out the north entrance and debated going the rest of the way around the island. As it often does here on sunny summer days, the midday wind had abated. It was around 4 P.M. and I was getting hungry for the meal at Rob and Jackie's place. I knew that we would be at least an hour or two getting back. We decided to head back the way we came, but stop at the main beach near the old pavilion. Gabriola Island was picturesque in the distance and the small ferry that services it could be seen just offshore. After pulling up at the main beach near the old pavilion on Newcastle Island, we went for a short walk and visited the museum, sandstone quarry and coffee shop.

During our first trip, Rob had been an extremely slow paddler and not very adept at paddling in a straight line. This surprised me as he has broad shoulders and strong arms. After leaving the main beach by the old pavilion, Rob shot by me and I had to work to catch up. I commented on this to Rob and he smiled back that he had figured out the knack of paddling. We saw other kayakers heading out as we got near the busy south end of Newcastle Island Passage.

We waited until a few motorboats went by and then crossed. Two-thirds of the way across Rob pointed to a bump in the water out in the Nanaimo Harbour and said, "Is that a bird?" It looked like driftwood to me but maybe it was moving. Most of our paddling isn't in a straight line. We go from "what's that" to "let's go in there" and explore lots of nooks and crannies. The bird turned out to be a very much alive, full-grown immature Bald Eagle that was waterlogged.

What to do? The eagle was riding low in the water and started using his wings as oars when we approached. He was a good distance from land and most of the shore was rocky and hard to climb out on or busy with people. One close look at that beak and I knew that I didn't want to pick up this huge, wet, heavy bird.

We decided to escort him back across Newcastle Island Passage to a secluded reef off Newcastle Island. We kept our boats about 10 feet apart and the bows even with the eagle. If he became anymore waterlogged and started to go down, I figured that we could help support him with a paddle between the two kayaks. As we started crossing Newcastle Island Passage a 20-foot motor boat had to slow down and detour around us. Next, a 40-foot sailboat was bearing down on us. We didn't budge and neither did it. I started to get nervous. The sailboat people saw the eagle and finally veered around us. We backed off as our slow swimmer neared the reef. I gave a triumphant shout as he climbed out of the water and stretched out his dripping wet six-foot wingspan to dry.

We turned around to head once more across the Newcastle Island Passage and saw that we had gathered quite an audience of assorted boaters. Soon we were loading the kayaks on the car. I pulled out my mini-binoculars and had a look at our friend. His wings were now folded down but he hadn't moved. How did the bird become waterlogged? That was the question on our minds. Had he hooked a salmon that was too heavy and couldn't let go quickly enough? Or had he just been young and inexperienced and made a miscalculation diving near the water?

Our paddle had only been about 6 or 7 km, but with hiking and all, I was ready for Rob's barbecuing and Jackie's cooking!

Guess which get washed and polished more often?

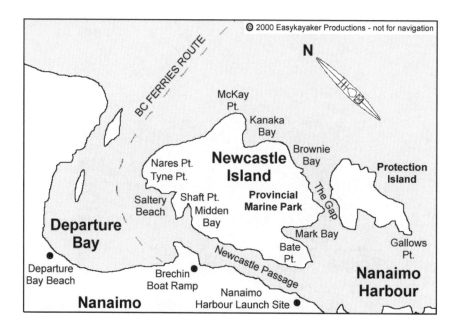

Chart #3443
Tidal Reference: Point Atkinson

Gary and Katherine testing a prototype for Nanaimo's silly boat race
Made of 6 mil poly and lots of tape

Brechin boat ramp—Nanaimo

The Brechin Boat Ramp is located on Zorkin Road in Nanaimo, within a stones throw of the Departure Bay ferry terminal. The boat ramp is adjacent to the Sealand public market and at first glance it looks like part of the parking lot for Sealand. Although it must be busy some days, we have never experienced any wait for launching or landing. There are two doublewide boat launches, one single boat launch and lots of (pay) parking.

One afternoon near Christmas we met at Jan and Dale's and sat before the glow of the fireplace looking at charts. I had a wild idea of paddling from Ladysmith to somewhere near Victoria, stopping at bed & breakfasts along the way. Eventually sense prevailed, and we decided that it would be too much paddling for the kids and both Paul's wife, Imelda, and my wife, Teesh.

What we finally planned for mid-summer was a three-family five-day kayak camping adventure in the Gulf Islands. However, even this Gulf Island adventure was going to be more paddling than these four were used to. So on a beautiful spring day, we decided to go for a shakedown group paddle and build up a few muscles and skills. I had ordered a new kayak for myself but it wouldn't be here for another week or so. That left us one boat short, so Teesh volunteered to stay home and pursue her favourite hobby of textile artistry (sewing).

This time of year, all the kayaks are kept on the trailer, unless they are in the water. Katherine, who was eleven at the time, and I loaded gear, hitched up the trailer to the Toyota and checked the tie-downs on the boats. We drove to Yellow Point and picked up Paul, Imelda and their eleven-year-old son Jordan.

When we arrived at the Brechin boat ramp in Nanaimo, I backed the trailer down to the water's edge and we unloaded. Dale and Jan arrived just as I bought a parking ticket. They quickly unloaded their Current Designs Solstice GT boats. Today Paul and Jordan were going to paddle a Necky Amaruk double kayak. Imelda would try a Current Designs Storm. This would be her first time paddling a single and using a rudder. Katherine would paddle what she now considered her boat, which was a Necky Narpa. I would be in my wooden Cape Charles.

This Cape Charles is a beautifully crafted home built boat. It has a slim Feathercraft rudder and a small skeg (miniature rear keel). Most of us keep the rudder up whenever possible to reduce drag. The problem with an up rudder is that it works like a steering sail, turning your boat into the wind. For this reason, some rudders like the Feathercraft are minimal in size. The Solstice and the Storm models use another solution to this problem. They have swept up bows which help balance out the rudder up / wind steering problem.

The Brechin boat ramp launch site is located near the north end of Newcastle Island Passage. Our plan involved the circumnavigation of Newcastle Island, a trip of about 10 km when you count the jogs and side trips. With a northerly breeze, we decided to head north into Departure Bay and use the wind to help us coast down the outside of the island. After launching, we quickly crossed Newcastle Island Passage to the shore of Newcastle Island and were at Midden Bay.

The name Midden Bay comes from the large midden near the abandoned native village site of Clostun. A midden, in reality, is an ancient refuse heap. This bay also saw a lot of coal mining activity from the early 1850s until the close of the Fitzwilliam Coal mine in 1883. Shaft Point is on the north end of the little bay. Paul's father had worked in the Number 1 and Northfield mines when he was seventeen. This had sparked an interest from Paul to recently write a school play, *Trapped by Coal*, and a children's book with the story centered around local mining. As we paddled Paul told us some interesting local history.

Once north of Shaft Point we entered Departure Bay and passed a gravel and sandy shore called Saltery Beach. Four Japanese-owned herring salteries once stood here in the late 1800s and early 1900s. One grew into a large shipyard named Nanaimo Shipyards Limited (around 1918), which in 1945 moved to the Nanaimo side at the south end of Newcastle Island Passage.

Paul and Imelda's son, Jordan, reminded us that were approaching a very dangerous area. After Tyne Point and Nares Point at the north end of Newcastle Island, cliffs and large rocks replace the beach. The ferry travels close to Newcastle here and to be caught in-between the ferry and the cliff or rocks can add a new meaning to the term "rock 'n' roll." Jordan suggested we might want to beach our boats until the next ferry went by.

The adults inopportunely, decided to ignore the wise advice of an eleven-year-old and to just paddle quickly around this potentially dangerous area. Of course, as soon as we started through the area, the ferry blew its loud piercing whistle to signal its departure. We paddled even faster and entered into the shadows of the cliffs. We were no longer protected from the wind and the waves were getting a little sloppy. Imelda was bringing up the rear and wasn't too sure she liked paddling a single kayak in these conditions. Waves kept hitting her bow at the wrong angle and splashing her. With the ferry coming, those in the lead stopped to allow the rear boats to catch up while giving strong words of encouragement. We all started again and the ferry came towering by as we rounded the north end of the island. We entered back into the sunshine and started to surf the waves south. We went further out from shore to prepare for the fun that would soon begin.

The wake from the ferry is a favourite among most of us. We wanted to be far enough out from the rocks to really enjoy surfing it. As the large wake-generated waves approached, we started to paddle fast enough to catch the ride. The Cape Charles has a straight bow, which stayed about three inches underwater as I rode several waves. At first this was a bit unnerving, but with the boat being over 18 feet long and having an inflated buoyancy bag in the bow, I felt quite safe from having the boat dive on me.

I looked over to see how my daughter was doing. She loves rough water and was in her element. Unfortunately, she was also surfing in the direction of a huge underwater reef that the wake was breaking over. I started yelling at her to turn and I paddled quickly her way. She turned in plenty of time to avoid riding up on the rocks, but as she was having so much fun, she didn't want to leave the waves too soon. Nonetheless, she gave me a scare.

The skeg on my boat really improves tracking and seldom did I need the rudder down. The problem with it is that you can't turn on a dime like smooth bottomed boats. The other aspect to the boat is that it is hard chimed. This means that instead of a curved hull, it has a series of flat planes. The end result is that the boat has good secondary stability (roll over prevention), but poor initial stability and was a hard boat to relax in when waves hit at certain angles. Once you got to know how stable it really was, you could have fun.

In no time we had reached Kanaka Bay. (See section on Nanaimo Harbour launch for more information on this bay and on Newcastle Island Provincial Marine Park.) The tide was out so most of the bay was dry. There was enough water to paddle in about 300 feet and pull up on the beach. As the tide would soon be coming in, we moved the boats quite a ways up from the waterline. We climbed up to a grassy knoll overlooking an incredible view and spread out our lunches.

I think we gain weight on these kayak trips. Everyone seems to bring enough food to feed the whole group. I had bought a bag of miniature peanut butter cups, which came along on about four trips until they were all used up. Jan had some grapes from the natural foods store that were the size of small plums and very tasty. Dale seemed to have brought every cheese known to man. We all had sandwiches, cookies and fruit juices. The sun was warm, Imelda's wet arms dried quickly, and comments flowed about how wonderful life was.

Several of us went for short walks on the beautiful trails that wind through giant trees near the bay. When I came back, Katherine and Jordan were practicing their hydrological engineering skills by constructing dams to keep the rising tide from entering parts of the bay. It was too nice to rush back to the boats, but the tide had risen up to them. They would float away if we didn't move them, so we decided to paddle on.

The rest of the way south was a free ride being gently pushed by the wind on our backs to what is known as "The Gap" between Newcastle and Protection Islands. Sheltered from the breeze, the water was almost mirror flat. We paddled in and around Mark Bay, rounded Bate Point and were at the south end of Newcastle Island Passage. The winds seemed to have freshened against us and the next 2 km didn't look to be easy paddling. Fortunately there weren't waves as this area doesn't have open expanses of water.

Paul and Jordan must have found their second wind as they took off like a rocket up the passage. Katherine pooped out and asked for a tow. Imelda had tired from fighting the head wind and slowed to a crawl. Dale and Jan were doing great; one was back visiting with Imelda and one was ahead of Paul and Jordan.

With Katherine in tow I crossed over to the Nanaimo side of the passage and started using the marinas for wind blocks. This worked great and we saw some very interesting large old boats. After a while, Katherine felt rested and we caught up with Paul and Jordan who were inspecting an ancient looking boat that must have been 80 feet in length. They borrowed the tow rope and paddled back to Imelda who gratefully accepted a tow back to the launch site.

Although not a West Coast wolf, you may see or
hear this fellow's cousins in some areas of
Vancouver Island.

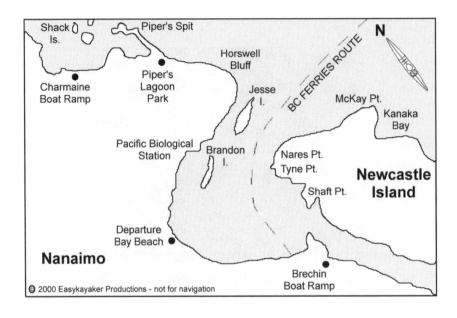

Chart #3443
Tidal Reference: Point Atkinson

Salmon heading upstream to spawn

Departure Bay to Piper's Lagoon—Nanaimo

Departure Bay is easily accessible from the old Island Highway that runs through Nanaimo. Look for the sign for Departure Bay Road. It's a little way north of Departure Bay Ferry Terminal. Turn onto Departure Bay Road and it's about a two minute drive to the beach and launch site.

Kayakers arriving by ferry from Vancouver's Horseshoe Bay Terminal into Nanaimo can see this launch site in a glance from the ferry's starboard side as the ferry docks. The ferry enters Departure Bay between Horswell Bluff and the tip of Newcastle Island. Jesse Island appears on the starboard side as the ferry enters the bay. Protected by a series of reefs, the Biological Station can be seen just beyond Jesse Island.

Keep to the right after driving off the ferry and turn up Brechin Hill Road. Stay in the right lane. As you near the top of the road take the right exit rather than keeping left with the main traffic. In another short block you will turn right onto Departure Bay Road. Follow Departure Bay Road past Brooks Landing (mall on left) to the bottom of the hill. A long beach will appear behind a concrete wall when you reach the launch site.

After several wonderful kayaking trips in the summer my busy work schedule took over the month of September. Heaped, thick clouds settled across East Vancouver Island in late September. Thoughts of summer kayaking had nestled into the far reaches of my mind as though the early fall winds had blown them there. But an e-mail message from Gary one Thursday evening stirred ideas of relaxation. One good day of weather was predicted for Sunday through satellite imagery and we were set.

Gary arrived promptly at 9:00 A.M. and I shoved my kayak gear bag into the back of his 4-wheel drive. My kayak was already fastened onto his kayak trailer with two other boats. Gary introduced me to two friends, Lois and Brian, who would paddle the short double kayak that Gary and I used before we upgraded to single kayaks. Being beamy and stable makes the double a great boat for beginners. We headed north through Yellow Point and Cedar and then toward Departure Bay to meet the rest of our kayaking team—Dale and Jan.

Everybody arrived at the beach almost at the same time. A crisp, sunny late-September morning glistened across a slightly windy, protected bay. "Yes!" I cried. I set up my kayak anxiously and was the first in the water. Soon the party of six paddled quietly along the north shore toward the Biological Station.

As we neared Jesse Island I told Jan a short story set in 1908 about a coal steamer named the Henrietta. Departure Bay had originally been a coal port. Many famous steamships and schooners had anchored or docked in the bay. Hamilton Powder Works (the Cilaire properties opposite Brooks Landing) overlooked the southern side of the shores. In Departure Bay proper, a sailors' hotel and bar as well as a jailhouse had once resided. Large steamers and ships unloaded their ballast near the Biological Station creating an artificial reef. Then they would take on a load of Wellington coal. Many original Nanaimo residents have picked a variety of rocks from this artificial reef.

In 1908 one relatively unknown steamer entered Departure Bay. Mules and horses destined to work in the coal mines were penned on deck. The Henrietta ill-navigated that July day, had beached itself onto a reef near Jesse Island. Fortunately, it was able to back off but onto another reef. The ship listed and the animals panicked. The crew tried to rescue the stricken, terrorized mules and horses. They untied them and the animals fled to the gunwale and jumped overboard. Many of the mules and horses died; several of them managed to swim to a small reef that protruded just above the water. However, the rising tide soon forced them to swim away. One animal apparently swam around Newcastle Island.

Today the winds were blowing from the northwest, which meant that the landmass was protecting us. The winds can really pick up in Departure Bay. On this day they barely bristled our hair. We kept close to shore and worked our way in and out of the coastline. Soon we rounded Horswell Bluff and headed toward Piper's Lagoon. It was quickly in view. To our right we could see Hudson Rocks and the faint outlines of seals or sea lions.

This area is open to the Strait of Georgia and as a result is subject to strong winds. As we paddled the winds increased. Several windsurfers were whipping around at quite a rapid speed out from Piper's Lagoon. This area is a haven for windsurfers due to its wind and waves.

Soon we were in the lee of Piper's spit. Fortunately, Piper's Lagoon had been made into a park several years ago. It had once been destined to be the home of a hotel complex or condominiums. Just metres north of the actual lagoon are the Shack Islands.

This was Lois' first time in a kayak and Brian's first time in the rear seat having to not only steer, but to also paddle in sync with Lois. We could see we would be in water that was quite rough if we were to continue around to the Shack Islands. Brian and Lois quickly agreed to stop in calm water for a rest.

We waited a few minutes in the lee before rounding a rough, rocky point. A family of four had hopscotched from the beach onto an outcropping of rock; the youngest child of 3 or 4 years old clutched her dad's hand, as she balanced precariously on a pinnacle of stone. The mother held the hand of her brother. We glided by unnoticed about 40 feet offshore.

Kayaking from Departure Bay to Piper's Lagoon is an easy paddle (about 9 km round trip). No one expected to strain their shoulder muscles or see open-crossing weather. As we ventured literally yards beyond the rocky point the wave action changed dramatically. A stiff northeasterly wind blew 5-foot waves onto the rocky beach below a 30-foot cliff. The waves bounced back and resulted in some seriously big waves (especially for Easykayakers!). For about 5 to 10 minutes we faced the roughest kayaking conditions that we had encountered in the past 2 years.

I was just ahead of Gary. He told me later that I was above his head and then suddenly in a trough below him. I called out, "Let's turn around." It didn't take much prompting. We soon spun about. Brian and Lois turned toward the rocks, the wrong move, but by the time I saw what was happening it was too late to shout to them to turn the other way. They were able to turn sharp enough to avoid being pounded by the surf into the rocks. A safe distance should be kept from the rocky beach in conditions like these to allow time for an assisted rescue from the other kayaks in the event of a capsize.

The rest of us turned away from the rocks and cliff. As we started back I noticed that Dale seemed to be headed out to sea, toward Vancouver. His foot had momentarily come off the rudder pedal and he was having trouble completing his turn. After a moment he was steering again and we grouped back together. Other than the two turning problems, the big waves were a lot of fun and a great ride!

Turning in seas this large is interesting as you are parallel to the waves for a moment and usually get to balance on the crest of a wave or two. All but Brian and Lois had paddled for an extended time parallel to large waves on the West Coast the previous month. We were now somewhat at home doing our high and low braces when broadsided by breaking waves.

We headed into a cove between two points where the wind and water were calm and landed on a beautiful small beach for lunch. The short-term excitement had made us hungry. Gary joked with Dale that he had just invented another cliché similar to "not playing with a full deck" or "having only one oar in the water." Now we could say that "he only has one foot on the rudder pedals."

As was becoming customary, everyone had a chef's spread appearing from their lunch bags. We shared different cheeses, cookies, and other delights as we washed our food down with juices. We leaned against the sun-bleached cedar and fir logs as the sun shone through a rare stand of Garry Oak trees. We chatted and joked and whittled away an hour.

After a stroll around the trails of Piper's Lagoon we launched our boats. With a stiff wind on our backs our trip back was effortless. Once back in Departure Bay, we paddled the other shore of Jesse Island, then detoured over to the Pacific Biological Station and to a few coves that we missed on the way out. We spoke briefly with crewmen aboard the Biological Station's research boat and also with various people out in their gardens or on their decks as we paddled by.

One thing to keep in mind when paddling the Departure Bay area is that the BC Ferries (understandably) does not enjoy having kayakers in their path. As the ferries tend to hug Newcastle Island, it is safer (for kayakers) to stay on the Brandon Island and Jesse Island side of Departure Bay. Surfing the wake from the ferry can be quite fun as long as you're not too close to the actual ship.

(Note: It's an easy trip from Departure Bay to Piper's Lagoon. The area from Stevenson Point to Piper's is open to the Strait of Georgia. It's best to go on this trip with a light Northeasterly (or no wind) and paddle into the wind. Keep close to shore, but a safe distance from rocks.)

Paddling Newcastle Channel with a beer keg on deck
but that's another story

Photo by Gary Dobrovolsky

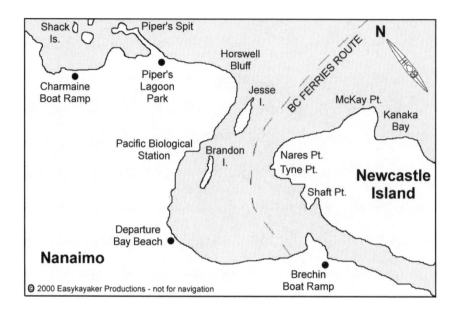

Chart #3443
Tidal Reference: Point Atkinson

Author
Paul Grey

Piper's Lagoon—Nanaimo

Piper's Lagoon is a beautiful park and walk. The lagoon and spit can be found north of Nanaimo off Hammond Bay Road. There are several ways to find Hammond Bay Road. One of the easiest ways is to take the Aulds Road exit off the Nanaimo Parkway. Aulds Road is near Home Depot, Staples, Costco and Woodgrove Mall. Once Aulds Road crosses the old Island Highway, it becomes Hammond Bay Road. Travel along Hammond Bay Road for almost seven kilometres. As you begin to near Piper's Lagoon and the Charmaine boat ramp, the Strait of Georgia becomes visible on your left. You will pass Piper's pub on your left before you see sparkling sea.

Charmaine Boat Launch is approximately 300 feet north of the lagoon turn off. You can park in the lot near the road or below by the boat ramp. This launch is your better choice during a low tide than Piper's Lagoon. It is also more sheltered than the lagoon launch site since it's partially protected by Hammond Bay.

If you are traveling north from downtown Nanaimo on the old Island Highway look for the Departure Bay Road turnoff after about 3 kilometres. There are two sets of lights in close proximity. The first takes you to the Departure Bay Ferry Terminal. Turn right at the second light onto Departure Bay Road and down a short, steep hill past the Brooks Landing Mall. Continue on the road to Departure Bay (on your right and very obvious). Just past the beach section as you're going up a hill make an immediate right turn onto Hammond Bay Road. Follow it for several kilometres. At one point the road will turn sharply left. The Piper's Lagoon turn off will be approximately ¾ kilometre past this sharp turn. There will be signs on the road for Piper's park.

When you turn right off Hammond Bay onto Lagoon Road you can drive straight ahead 300 feet from a small turnabout. You will have to check on tides for this launch or expect to walk quite far with your kayaks or canoes. Another option is to take the first (and only) right off Lagoon Road. Follow it for an approximate ½ kilometre to a parking lot. Park as close as you can to the gate, it's a popular spot on hot, weekend days. Expect to carry your boats a reasonable distance. If you picked a higher tide you can launch in the lagoon and head north toward Neck Point. You can also launch from the southerly side of Piper's spit.

Piper's Lagoon is rich in local history and exquisite in natural beauty. I have a special connection to the area through my father's family. I've visited and walked the spit and rugged shores a hundred times with friends, girlfriends, and now my wife and son.

Stories from my father, recently deceased, remain strong in my memory. My dad, born in Nanaimo, November 1921, lived part of his boyhood at Piper's Lagoon next, in fact, to the Piper family. Originally, only a rough trail or road wound its way from Departure Bay to Hammond Bay. My dad often remarked that it was easier to travel by canoe to Nanaimo than by horse before the road was improved. Dad spent many days fishing by boat with his father and fishing on his own from the local rocky shores nearby.

My Great Uncle Ned, now in his 90's, married Grace Piper. Apparently, she had inherited ¼ of the Piper estate (a large chunk of the fabulous Hammond Bay area). Unfortunately, they sold the property later for a small amount of money (once you see the area you'll know how valuable and beautiful it is). My uncle now lives in a home for the elderly and can still tell a good yarn about early Nanaimo and its coal mining days.

Today, we decided to launch from Charmaine Boat launch, accessible directly from Hammond Bay Road. Gary and I unloaded our kayaks on the paved boat access. The wind blew briskly and large waves rolled into Hammond Bay. We could hear the steady roar of gale force winds. Protected from the gusts of wind by the Shack Islands (aptly named after shacks on the islands) we were able to launch without bumping our boats too much on the boat ramp.

The shacks are now summer homes or get-a-ways for local people. During the depression in the 1930's many local people could not afford to pay taxes so they built lean-tos, shacks, and small houses on these islands. The islands are accessible on a low tide. Vi Henderson's book *Piper's Lagoon* offers good details about the islands. A whaling station was located just north of Piper's.

As we prepared to launch, a very young family of kayakers arrived with 3 boats: 2 small, river-type kayaks and a wood-constructed ocean kayak. They were going to play in the shallow sheltered waters south of our launch. We slipped into our kayaks and paddled away from shore while the mom and dad secured their children's life jackets and sprayskirts.

Gary and I paddled in the same direction as a large flock of Canada Geese was headed. The geese were not alarmed at our presence though they paddled quickly to maintain a safe distance. We followed a group of geese respectfully around a point of land to examine the various shacks. The group of geese quickly backtracked to their main flock—they stick together in the air, water or on land!

Gary's arm was sore from some recent forestry work, the waves rolling into Hammond Bay were very large and slightly intimidating, so we initially decided to limit our jaunt to paddling around the bay. We had picked too low a tide to scoot into the lagoon and the weather was too rough to venture far along the outside coastline.

The waves are often quite high in this area. Gary and I finally paddled out to the opening of Hammond Bay in order to surf our kayaks back into Hammond Bay. The wave troughs were deep and wide so we turned easily. When you're surfing, the trick is to get your kayak moving fast enough to go with the momentum of the waves. You have to power paddle rapidly to stay on the crest and not be pulled backwards. But once you get going is it ever fun! We flew into shore in just a few minutes! It's an unnerving feeling on the crest of a large wave when surfing for the first few times. Your rudder is out of the water and the boat feels quite tippy.

Gary and I are quite comfortable now in surfing conditions after doing a pool session with Brian from Pacific Northwest Expeditions. Gary and I are not big risk takers. We prefer to be knowledgeable and comfortable within our skill levels. While kayaking is incredibly safe and fun, you have to have basic knowledge about safety and rescue. We always recommend practicing bracing and getting back into your kayak safely (see Easykayaker safety tips).

If you're going to travel north along the outside coast from Piper's or Charmaine boat ramp, check on wind direction first. You can always find weather conditions from the Easykayaker website (www.easykayaker.com) by checking on the Reference Page or clicking a weather link. It would be advisable to start your paddle traveling into the wind and return with a stiff breeze on your back—easy sailing, of course!

Today was perhaps our shortest kayak adventure. We barely got our kayaks wet. I decided to buy a neoprene skirt instead of my basic nylon one (around $106.00 Cdn). One good wave and you're soaked from the waist down in a loose fitting nylon skirt. Well, we satisfied the basic urge to get out on the water and knew we had many great days ahead of us. As we drove away we could see the wind blowing the children in their kayaks into the shoreline with dad yelling out helpful directions. The kids seemed to be having fun and were very safe in water only a few inches deep.

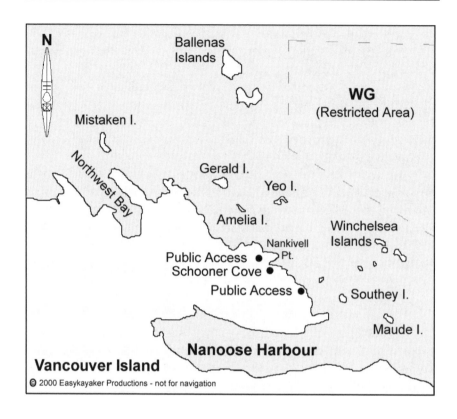

Chart #3512
Tidal Reference: Point Atkinson

Photo by Jan Pullinger

Schooner Cove—Nanoose

Schooner Cove is an oceanfront golf resort and marina about halfway between Nanaimo and Parksville. Northwest Bay Road meets the Island Highway just north of Nanoose Bay. There is a large gas station and traffic light at the intersection. Turn onto Northwest Bay Road, cross the railroad tracks and turn right onto Powder Point Road. Powder Point Road becomes Fairwinds Drive after a few kilometres and later becomes Dolphin Drive. Follow the signs to Schooner Cove, which is about a 20-minute drive from the highway turnoff. You will pass through the Fairwinds golf course just before you reach Schooner Cove.

We have used two launch sites in Schooner Cove, one just north of the cove via a public access trail and the other at Schooner Cove Marina. The marina has a small launching fee but it's a more convenient place to launch from than the other location. SeaDog Sailing and Kayaking offers kayak rentals and guide services from the marina.

To find the public access launch site, go past Schooner Cove on Dolphin Drive, take the first right (Schooner Drive, which becomes Blueback Drive) and look for Tyee Crescent. The access on Tyee is very close to where it intersects with Blueback. The access trail runs through the twisted blackberries to a shaded, rocky beach. Parking is easy, as there is plenty of room on the road shoulder beside the trail.

Today we decided to launch from the public access just north of Schooner Cove and Nankivell Point. We had to be careful launching here because of the barnacle-covered rocks and boulders. The small bay however was reasonably protected from winds. I was a little nervous today because I had seriously injured my lower back and this was a trial run before a longer trip to the Broken Group Islands. Fortunately, Gary (who is also subject to back problems) took the brunt of lifting and carrying our kayaks to the water's edge.

We began paddling in ideal, early August summer conditions to the western islands of the 16-island archipelago. The western islands consist of Yeo, Amelia, Gerald, and Mistaken. I felt quite strong paddling so Gary and I headed toward Amelia Island. We stopped paddling for a few minutes to visit with some fellow paddlers and then continued on. We reached the shores of Amelia Island in just over a half hour from our launch.

We noticed a large group of seals slipping into the water from Amelia but didn't think much about it until a group of around 40 seals were popping their heads up behind our boats as close as 5 metres (16 ft.) away. They kept up with us as we paddled along. Each time we turned our heads to look at them, they submerged into the crystal green waters that shimmered in the sun. Gary and I smiled at having such a large group of seals observing us so freely and acting as an escort. Perhaps in the spirit of their playfulness and innocence, we paddled gently, just barely cutting the water's surface, and floated along in a silence with only the sound of small waves breaking on a rock-strewn beach from some distant boat.

We kayaked along the north shore of Yeo for some time quietly watching our escort of seals and looked for spots to alight onto a beach. When we reached the end of Yeo we could see a second group of seals launch from their perch. Our adopted herd of seals suddenly disappeared into the depths of the Strait of Georgia and likely headed back to their sunning grounds. I briefly pondered whether the two herds of seals had their own territorial waters.

We circumnavigated the end of Yeo and found a large bay with a good pebble beach. We left our kayaks, tied them above high water mark, and walked along a narrow trail inspecting the plant types. Gary, a self-taught naturalist, was quite curious about one type of tall flowering plant and noted that he would look it up when he got home.

We would have island hopped to Mistaken Island but I decided not to push the injury in my back. So instead of Mistaken Island, we headed toward the Wincheleas Islands group for Schooner Cove Marina and arrived there within 40 minutes. We paddled around the docks and ran into a group of novice kayakers trying out their first day on the water. We saw Cliff Hermann, the owner of SeaDog, and chatted briefly with him. Gary had earlier chartered his sailboat to take himself, his wife and daughter, to Jedediah Island for a 5-day trip.

After a few easy minutes of gliding under ramps, around docks and past fancy sailboats we headed back to our launch site. We had discovered the beauty and charm of the area and looked forward to returning on another summer day to go island hopping either to the Winchelsea or Ballenas Island groups.

Section 9—Other Vancouver Island Paddles

Looking toward the church at
Friendly Cove on Nootka Island

Photo by Jan
Pullinger

Lunch on the Tiny Group in the Broken Group Islands

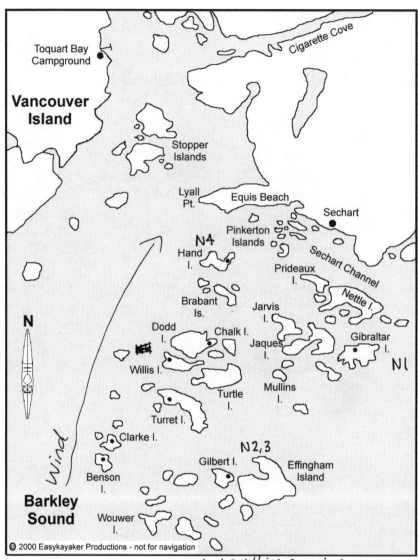

Toquart Bay
Campground

**Vancouver
Island**

Cigarette Cove

Stopper
Islands

Lyall
Pt.

Equis Beach

Sechart

Pinkerton
Islands

N4

Hand
I.

Prideaux
I.

Sechart Channel

Nettle I.

Brabant
Is.

Jarvis
I.

N

Dodd
I.

Chalk I.

Jaques
I.

Gibraltar
I.

Willis I.

N1

Turtle
I.

Mullins
I.

Turret I.

Clarke I.

Wind

N2,3

Gilbert I.

Effingham
Island

Benson
I.

**Barkley
Sound**

Wouwer
I.

© 2000 Easykayaker Productions - not for navigation

best paddling: mornings
Wind: afternoons
dark: 9:30pm

Chart #3670 scale 1:20,000
        or
Chart #3671 scale 1:40,000
Tidal Reference: Tofino

The Broken Group Islands—Barkley Sound

The Broken *Group* Islands are in Barkley Sound on Vancouver Island's West Coast. There is also a set of islands on the eastside of Vancouver Island called the Broken Islands.

I know why we keep coming back to the Broken Group Islands. It's a magical, wonderful, beautiful place of sheltered waters and old growth forests with a West Coast flavour. To me, paddling and camping in this area is a benchmark that I compare all my other trips to.

We recommend Mary Ann Snowden's book, *Island Paddling*, to anyone wishing to paddle this area without a guide. It's full of information about the Broken Group Islands. We also strongly recommend having chart #3670, a good compass and knowing how to use them both.

****

Trip 1

One of my first kayaking camping adventures was with an outfitter to the Broken Group. I was new to kayaking and my paddling had been limited to Vancouver Island's Gulf Islands and eastern shoreline. This was to be my first West Coast kayak adventure.

After a night's camping at Toquart Bay, we had a quick breakfast, packed our gear into the kayaks and had a short, easy paddle to the Stopper Islands. The narrow waterway between the Stoppers is quite pretty and very sheltered. Next we crossed over near Lyall Point. It's best for inexperienced paddlers to avoid making this 2 km crossing mid-afternoon when the winds come up. From Lyall Point we headed for Hand Island to have lunch and do a bit of exploring. After lunch we paddled through the Brabants around the outside of Dodd and landed at the incredibly beautiful beach on Willis Island. We had been going against a headwind for much of our 14 km trip and the last stretch around Dodd Island was not only windy, but also rough. We set up camp at Willis and I went for a swim.

This was to be the only rough water we would see on our trip. The Broken Group Islands offer many sheltered waterways, but some of the channels and the outward coast of the outside islands are affected by afternoon summer winds. Our guides took us in these areas during the calm mornings and we stayed to the more sheltered areas during the afternoons.

The next day we paddled around the outside of Willis to Lovett, and then around Clark and Benson enjoying the gentle ocean swells. It was my first time paddling in swells. They are very gentle to paddle compared to chop or wind waves. They can be hazardous though as a rock that is two feet under the surface one moment may be two feet above the surface a moment later. Another concern is that when paddling close to rocky shores, waves reflecting back can combine with incoming waves causing a much larger unexpected wave.

Later, we paddled to Turret and Turtle Islands and back to Willis for another night. We were all a little tired after 19 km but the excitement of paddling in the wide-open Pacific Ocean was still with us.

The third morning, we packed up camp and headed to Keith and Mullins Islands, around Dempster to look at the sea caves and over to Gibraltar for lunch. After lunch we paddled to Hand Island to camp. We had paddled 16 km. Our last morning had us heading through the Stoppers and back to Toquart Bay, a trip of 7 km that was over too soon. The abundant marine life, beautiful deserted beaches and huge rainforest trees that hung over some of the waterways created an experience that can't be adequately described. A group photo was taken on the beach. Suddenly, it was time to leave, but no one seemed to be in a hurry to do so. The weather had been kind to us; no rain and only a small amount of morning fog one day.

Trip 2

A couple of years later Jan, Dale, Paul and I headed to Toquart Bay. This would be their first trip to the Broken Group. We didn't camp at Toquart Bay so our launch time was around noon, but we were lucky and didn't have much wind for our crossing between the Stoppers and Lyall Point. We took a circuitous route exploring every rock and crevasse along the way to Willis Island, a paddling style soon adopted for most future trips. We never go the shortest way if there is some interesting shoreline to explore nearby (and "nearby" is very subjective).

We spent three nights at Willis Island, which we had almost to ourselves. Each day we would set the crab trap and then paddle off to explore in a new direction, eventually covering every foot of coastline of all the islands in the area surrounding Willis Island. We kept things to an Easykayaker pace, with late morning starts and only about 12 to 15 km of paddling a day. One day we returned just before dusk and began to cook dinner including our crab catch. We managed to get dinner cooked just before dark but ended up eating our crab in the dark. That was a challenge. We wore crab, butter, lemon and garlic to bed that night.

The trip back through the Pinkertons was wonderful. This is a very sheltered area of narrow, enchanting, winding waterways outside of the park. We had lunch at nearby Equis Beach. Conditions had been mirror-like on the water until we got in the kayaks after lunch and headed for Lyall Point and the subsequent crossing to the Stoppers. The afternoon winds were blowing straight in from the Pacific and the largest wind waves that we had ever paddled in were broadsiding us. Our boats were loaded with gear, which made them very stable. We tucked our chins down and headed across. No one said much, but all four of us were actually enjoying it and experimenting with our paddles.

Occasionally a wave would break higher and water would wash across the top of our boats. The sprayskirts did their job and we stayed dry. Most of our trip had almost been too tame. We did adventure to the outside of Dodd one afternoon for a rock 'n' roll ride, but the rest of our paddling had been in very calm water and seldom required our rudders down.

Trip 3

A year later the same group as well as John and Sue launched from Toquart about 11 A.M. We paddled through the Stoppers, to Lyall Point and over to Equis Beach for lunch. After lunch we went through the Pinkertons, between Prideaux and Nettle Islands, by Erin Island and over to Gibraltar. This was John and Sue's first kayak camping trip. They were paddling a double that is cooperatively owned by eight couples. The double had been my first kayak and instead of selling it, we "co-op"ed it.

With the long August weekend ending we were certain Gibraltar Island and the Broken Group would be crowded but Gibraltar was almost deserted and we hardly saw a soul during day paddling. It's the closest campsite to where the Lady Rose docks at Sechart and subsequently a favourite camping spot. We set up camp and had a wonderful meal cooked by John. We are now in the habit of each person taking turns making a gourmet group supper, but we look after our own breakfasts and lunches.

For the next few days we explored all the local islands, islets, rocks and reefs. We paddled in the swells on the outside during the mornings and in the sheltered waterways the rest of the day. On our last full day, the Lady Rose brought many more kayakers to the Broken Group and our peaceful beach became crowded and noisy with the excitement of children. We hauled in our crab traps and were surrounded with children and a few adults as we measured the crabs. By 8 P.M. the beach was quiet again and appeared deserted.

One thing I've never been too concerned about is crowded campsites. On the whole kayakers are great people and are quite considerate when camping. Most days we spend our time kayaking and visiting deserted beaches, during which time we'd rarely see another kayak. Gibraltar has a long beach and the camping is spread over a good-sized area.

The next day, our trip back was timed to miss the afternoon winds.

The three hours that I had been up had been quite foggy. Jaques, the nearest island would appear and disappear. Finally we were off. Our plan that day was to follow Jaques, Jarvis, travel to the Brabants and then over to Hand Island to explore and have lunch.

The fog thickened as we left. I was able to use the chart and a visual sighting to line up a couple of rocks to get a good compass bearing. Jan and I each had our GPS's switched on. We had played with the GPS's before but this was our first time in thick fog. Even on a clear day the hundred or so islands, islets and rocks can confuse us if we don't track every turn on our charts.

An hour later the fog lifted and Hand Island became visible. The tide was just high enough to take the shortcut across Hand's peninsula and swing around onto the main beach. My GPS said we were within 300 metres. Since then Jan got me using calipers to scale the charts to the nearest second for programming the GPS. We explored Hand Island and checked out campsites for future visits. We snacked but weren't ready for lunch.

Hand's beach and campsite are wonderful, but sometimes crowded. There's a lot of room for camping and it's an easy paddling distance (7.5 km) to Toquart Bay. Should you want to stop at the Stoppers (sorry, couldn't resist), there's a great little beach on the southeast side of South Stopper behind a couple of small islets. We enjoyed stopping there for lunch. Had it not been for the threat of the afternoon winds, I would have loved paddling over to explore Cigarette Cove and visit the lodge there.

We landed at Toquart around 2 P.M. and enlisted a nearby camper to take our traditional group photo. As we started our drive out the afternoon winds picked up.

Trip 4—Broken Group Islands via M.V. Frances Barkley

We arrived at the dockside in Port Alberni at 7:00 A.M. Unloading quickly we soon had our kayaks situated near the M.V. Frances Barkley and a large plastic tote filled to the brim with camping gear and kayak equipment (one tote is good for 2 kayakers). The M.V. Lady Rose, sistership to the Barkley, sat tied to a nearby dock. With our tickets in hand we soon found out we had arrived on perhaps the busiest Monday morning of the year. Our kayaks were carried onto the ship by friendly crew and were packed carefully on deck.

The Barkley, a former Norwegian ferry boat, has a length of 128 feet and a beam of 24 feet, and now serves as a freight ship and ferry from Port Alberni to the West Coast of Vancouver Island. She can carry 200 passengers and 100 tons of cargo. The ship is reasonably comfortable to sail on though it can be crowded on peak summer runs.

One and a half hours later we sailed unceremoniously through the

Port Alberni inlet to Barkley Sound. Spectacular West Coast forests lined the inlet from shore to mountainside. On this journey we were treated to the sight of a mother bear and her cub scouring a rocky outcropping for a bivalve meal. Significant, annual rainfalls feed the streams and rivers in this area. According to Environment Canada (1998), Victoria received 85.8 cm (34 inches) of precipitation on average from 1961 – 1990, Port Alberni received 188.6 cm (75 inches), and Tofino received 323.6 cm (131.4 inches). Apparently, there are areas in the inlet that receive even more rain. The Barkley Sound area is unarguably rainforest.

Day 1—Sechart Lodge

Before we landed at the Sechart Lodge, a crewmember reviewed safety tips for traveling in the Broken Group Islands. Much of the information was common sense but it was a good reminder for kayakers on basic safety tips. He reminded us how easy it is to get disorientated in the Broken Group and let us know charts were available on board for purchase. We talked to the rest of the kayakers as to where they were planning to camp and we decided to camp at Willis Island or Clarke—both have campsites that face the setting sun. Once the ship landed all the kayakers were called to the top of the dock. Two Park Wardens spoke to us about the various campsites and again reviewed safety tips for the area.

The next hour seemed chaotic but it was fun for some. Kayakers were incoming and kayakers were outgoing. The small dock area was filled with totes, kayaks, and gear spread out everywhere. It was then that Gary experienced his one and only near disaster of the trip. Someone emptied out half his tote and he had to scramble around quickly before his equipment and supplies were packed away. Fortunately, Gary loads his kayak systematically and knew what was missing.

Our group this trip was a party of ten people. It was enjoyable having such a large group of interesting people—good food and interesting conversations. While waiting for the last of our group to launch, those of us in the water paddled over to look for signs of the old Sechart Whaling Station. The whaling station operated from 1905 to 1917. Today only a few fruit trees, pilings, and shrubs remain.

There are two easy routes to enter the Pacific Rim National Park from the Sechart Lodge; paddle west through the Pinkerton Islands, and to Hand Island or kayak south past Canoe Island and across to Prideaux Island. Either route requires a crossing of Sechart Channel, which can be subject to winds blowing from either the northwest or southeast. We paddled in calm, open water conditions making the 1.4 km crossing headed for Prideaux Island.

Our pace slowed deliberately as we paddled between Prideaux and

Nettle and around the east side of Denne Island and then headed toward the sheltered waters between Jaques and Jarvis Islands. In the special narrow channels between the islands, the beauty and tranquility of the Broken Group is revealed. With draping moss-laden branches stretching toward the water, a kayaker, splitting the silence with only the stroke of a paddle, enters a world of calm and into the past of the Nuu-chah-nulth Peoples.

There are dozens of locations where the First Nations lived or fished. Middens, an ancient refuse heap, are very easy to spot in some locations. The Nuu-chah-nulth deposited the shells of clams, oyster, mussels and the bones of other sea-faring animals onto the ground often right behind their homes. Over a period of hundreds of years the shells and bones pulverized and formed middens.

In the sheltered area between Jaques and Jarvis Islands are two stone fish traps and a canoe run that were used long ago by the First Nations People. The location appears ideal to trap fish. Aboriginal people in cedar-dug canoes, would wave cedar branches under the water to direct oolichan or herring toward the entrapment. Once fish were hoarded into the enclosure the opening would be closed off and they would wait for the tide to fall. The Nuu-chah-nulth Peoples lived on a rich diet of seafood. They also supplemented their diet with whales, seals, sea lions, and other sea animals.

From the sheltered area we paddled through the Tiny Group, past Chalk Island and toward the protected waters between Turtle, Walsh, Dodd and Willis Islands. We landed at Willis Island and after a quick look at the available campsites, decided to call it home for the next few days.

Day 2—Clarke and Benson Islands

The next morning there were some long faces when Dale, Jan, Brett, Tina, Kees and Jessica learned that their breakfast and lunch bags were not with us. Jan had a VHF radio and we learned from other kayakers that Sechart Lodge monitored VHF calls on channel 6. It turned out that the group that had raided Gary's gear had also struck Jan and Dale.

Our group launched mid-morning after breakfast and headed on a southeast beat around Willis Island into Thiepval Channel. We usually planned our days to cross the windy channels in the morning or very late afternoon (we are Easykayakers of the laid-back sort). Thiepval, subject to strong winds, was calm so we paddled straight across to Trickett Island. The fog was fairly thick and we were not within site of land for most of our paddling from Willis to Lovett. Navigation was by compass and GPS.

The next crossing was over to Owens Island and across on the outside to Clarke. Clarke and Benson are enchanting islands bestowed with open meadows, trails, and the remains of a turn-of-the-century hotel. Benson has a blowhole that can be quite exciting on its outer shore. Our group landed on the beach-campsite at Clarke and we traipsed around the island inspecting the beaches, the homesite, and trails. Our visit was short because we wanted to get to Benson Island for a tour of the archeological dig. This was to be the last day of the dig and the next day they would be filling in the open trench.

We landed on a beach just north of the Benson campsite to eat our lunch. As we sat down, Kees, a Dutch member of our group, remarked that they didn't have logs on the beaches in Holland. Our beaches are crisscrossed with logs of cedar, hemlock, and fir—common fixtures on the West Coast. I asked him what they had on their beaches and he replied, "We have sticks and some things that wash in." I began my lunch appreciating the log I was leaning on.

The archeological tour began at 2:00 P.M. The Sheshaht speaker gave us an account of the local First Nations history and then gave us a tour of a dig on a lower elevation toward the beach. The dig, shored with WCB approved supports was quite deep. The most exciting discovery of the day was a mussel-tip harpoon imbedded in a piece of whale skull bone. Most of the workers at the site were Nuu-chah-nulth youth. Their spirits seemed high. Apparently Benson Island had been fogged in much of the summer and today was their first sunny day. This area gets more fog than the rest of the Broken Group, which is one reason we don't usually choose to camp at Clarke, Benson or Gilbert.

Part way back to camp the afternoon winds picked up and we found a nearby beach to enjoy until wind and sea conditions calmed.

Day 3

After a late morning start on day 3, we decided on a less strenuous trip around Turtle, the Tiny Group, Mullins, and Onion Island. The highlight of the day turned out to be eating rather than kayaking. I'm a vegetarian at home but on outings I eat some meat. In the midst of the Tiny Group is a beautiful, white shell-crushed beach. We pulled our kayaks from the water and quickly donned our swimming gear. The water was quite warm.

Then the food extravaganza began—Dutch specialty sausage, smoked oysters, kippers, Cowichan cheese, Dutch cheese, bagels with 3 types of cream cheese, bannock with homemade blackberry jam, tortilla chips, and a splattering of other foods. Albert was cooking hotdogs over a small fire. The hotdogs took a little longer to cook and by the time he offered us his fare the comments were beginning, "Ohhh, I can't eat any more."

After the gourmet lunch our group split in two: some members headed to Mullins and Onion Island and others decided to kayak slowly back to camp exploring Chalk Island on the way.

By early evening the sky had darkened with thick, cumulus clouds.

Our fire fueled by imported Benson Island wood, warmed us while we drank hot chocolate. We had set up a tarp for protection from the expectant rain. The evening set in much earlier and most members soon headed toward their respective tents. I read a novel by headlamp and slowly fell asleep. The rains fell throughout the late night. I woke up several times to a sudden pounding of water on my overhead tarp. I quickly nodded off each time with the quiet knowledge that I had waterproofed my tent for this trip!

Day 4

It appeared everyone had awakened several times throughout the night because it was a slow-rising crew. The clouds were low lying and threatening to rain again. Almost by proxy vote we decided to read in our tents or sit beside a new fire and chat. It was a day we all felt like taking it easy. A doe and spotted fawn visited our campsite and grazed within 10 feet of us. Jackie and Albert added to the beach's stone sculptures with a beautifully crafted inukshuk. During the late afternoon a calm settled over the area and we paddled around Dodd Island. Thanks to Albert we had a fabulous crab feed for supper.

Day 5—Return to Sechart Lodge

On the final morning we monitored the weather channel and found out that a storm resided over northern Vancouver Island and also in Juan De Fuca Strait; we appeared to be sandwiched between two weather fronts with winds that were supposed to pick up around noon.

We decided to get to the lodge by 12:00 P.M. for a shower and to avoid the human traffic. This would prove to be a fortuitous decision. On the journey back we were treated to two river otters surfacing and chewing a fish together until they spotted us. Later in the Pinkerton Islands we passed an Elder Hostel Group outfitted and guided by Sealegs Kayaking—everyone seemed to be very happy!

When we arrived at the docks the Frances Barkley had just unloaded the latest batch of kayakers and there wasn't room on the floats for our kayaks. After waiting approximately 15 minutes some space opened up and we took turns unloading and lifting our boats onto the dock. We worked as a team and soon everyone headed towards the showers at the day lodge. Not long after our showers (operated by loonies), a huge line-up of people formed with the same idea. We bought cold beer from the lodge, relaxed and waited for the M.V. Frances Barkley to return from Ucluelet.

Due to the rain during the return trip to Port Alberni, the ship's interior was more crowded than on our last trip. People seemed to be crammed into every nook and cranny available. I decided that when I return next time to the Broken Group, it wouldn't be in August and if by ship, I wouldn't travel on a Monday or Friday. But who's complaining? In my mind's eye I can still remember the last mid-morning day near Dodd Island in perfectly calm waters, the sun, surrounded by a thin veil of clouds, reflected softly in the water surrounded by a surreal circle of blue sky. I guided myself quietly along by the shimmering image feeling peaceful and knowing why I loved kayaking.

****

Broken Group Wildlife

Marine life is plentiful within the Broken Group. Seals can be seen throughout the islands, but to see the sea lion colonies you may need to visit Wouwer Island. I have a lot of respect for sea lions and although they're not known to attack kayakers, their threatening gestures, when you paddle too close, are enough for me. One morning while sitting on Willis's beach we were treated to a visit by a sea lion and a porpoise. The porpoise announced his arrival by making some loud unique noises to let us know the show was about to begin. Out came our four pair of mini-binoculars and we watched the porpoise perform what looked like circus tricks. Another time, on Nettle Island, while sitting on a beautiful sandy beach we had a close encounter with a large river otter that walked from the woods through our picnic to the water as if we weren't there. It was a treat to see one on land so close up. Once, many years ago, when onboard the Lady Rose between the Broken Group and Ucluelet we drifted for a while alongside a small pod of whales and later while motoring among the Broken Group we saw a buck deer swimming between islands.

Bird life is also abundant. Bald eagles are everywhere. Not a day of paddling goes by without seeing many of these majestic birds. At our campsite on Gibraltar we watched an eagle swoop down with talons extended into the water to catch something, but it missed. The eagles are so used to kayakers that they are easily viewed close up. Herons, gulls and smaller sea birds are also plentiful. Crows will get into your food if you give them the slightest chance.

On land, camp-robbing squirrels will visit you and at night the mice come out to wander around. My last tent was dome shaped and on Willis Island every night a mouse would try to climb up the outside of the tent only to get part way up and slide all the way down. Fortunately the mice are not the type that try to chew into everything. One night we left a tall coffee mug with some sweet drink residue in it with plans to wash it in the morning light. The next morning we had a very sticky mouse that needed help to climb out of the cup.

Mink are abundant on the islands and we've watched them both from camp as they walk along the waterline at low tide and from our boats as we paddled. Raccoons are also common, but I've never seen one in the Broken Group. Each morning while camping at Willis Island there were sandy raccoon prints on our kayaks, and we saw many mouse, mink, raccoon and deer tracks in the wet sand.

The blacktailed deer are used to people on the islands and you often see them in the morning or evening. One night when asleep in my tent, sandwiched between a large driftwood log and a wall of salal, I was awakened buy a quiet sound only inches away that I couldn't identify. After laying there for a minute or so I became completely baffled (which isn't hard to do when woken up at 2 A.M.). I decided to make some noise myself and see what happened. The next thing I heard was the clatter of hooves on the driftwood log as the deer that was chewing his cud next to my ear bounded away. The next morning I was the first one up (I'm an early riser). I sat on the log, fired up my one-burner Coleman, made oatmeal and hot chocolate, ate the oatmeal and was drinking my HC when a buck came walking down the beach toward me. The bow of my boat was next to me as I sat on the log and the deer was walking toward the stern of my boat. I sat motionless; I could feel the breeze gently on my face, so I knew my scent was going away from the deer. As he sniffed my rudder (about 18 ft. away) I must have moved. The buck literally leaped into the air and took off at quite a clip. An hour later while walking down the beach, three of us paused to watch a doe and her fawn graze on the brush at the edge of the sand.

****

Words from Parks Canada

There are eight designated camping areas in the Broken Group Islands within national park boundaries, located on Hand, Turret, Gibraltar, Willis, Dodd, Clarke, Benson and Gilbert Islands. All island visitors and users must camp in these designated campsites. Random campers will be asked to move to one of the designated campsites. Camping in areas other than designated campsites is a violation under various Acts that will be enforced as appropriate.

All the campsites are small and cannot sustain large groups. Maximum stay on each island campsite is four (4) days. Maximum stay in the Broken Group Islands is fourteen (14) days. Solar composting outhouses are provided at the campsites.

Some campsites are located near small, seasonal streams, but during summer months, fresh water is very hard to find. Any water from island sources should be boiled or treated before drinking. It is suggested that all boaters bring an adequate drinking water supply with them into the Broken

Group Islands.

Be campfire free. Previous campers have created serious vegetation damage seeking firewood. If you must have a fire, build it only on beaches below the high-tide line and use only driftwood. All fires must be out after use and fire debris cleaned up.

There is no garbage pick-up in the islands. Visitors must pack out whatever they pack in. Fishing must comply with Department of Fisheries and Oceans regulations. Dogs and pets disturb wildlife and interfere with other visitors' enjoyment of the wilderness. Please leave pets at home.

****

A last but important note from Easykayaker is that although excellent clean outhouses are provided at the designated camping areas on the islands, toilet paper is not. We ran into a party of five adults and four kids planning to stay six days. They had one roll of toilet paper. Let's see, that's how many squares per person per day? We gave them most of our extra paper the day we left.

Nettle Island in
the Broken
Group

Photo by
Jan Pullinger

Sea cave on
the outside of
Dempster
Island

Photo by
Sue Little

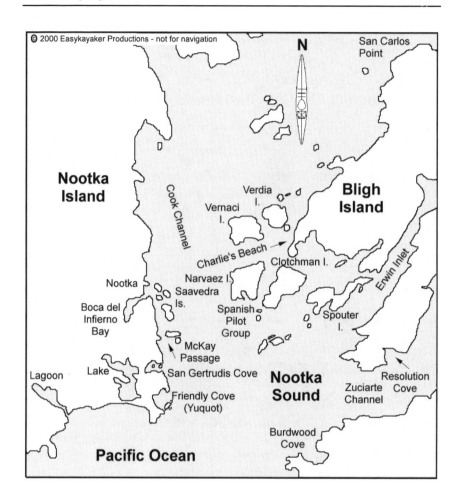

© 2000 Easykayaker Productions - not for navigation

N

San Carlos
Point

**Nootka
Island**

Cook Channel

Verdia
I.

Vernaci
I.

**Bligh
Island**

Charlie's Beach

Clotchman I.

Erwin Inlet

Nootka

Narvaez I.

Saavedra
Is.

Boca del
Infierno
Bay

Spanish
Pilot
Group

Spouter
I.

Lagoon   Lake

McKay
Passage

San Gertrudis Cove

**Nootka
Sound**

Resolution
Cove

Zuciarte   Channel

Friendly Cove
(Yuquot)

Burdwood
Cove

Pacific Ocean

Chart #3675
Tidal Reference: Tofino

Hoisted onto the
MV Uchuck III

Nootka Sound, Spanish Pilot Group, Friendly Cove

Lured by another West Coast kayaking adventure to an area we hadn't yet paddled, I hadn't quite realized how rich the history of Nootka Sound and area would be. After five days of kayaking, hiking, and site touring, my imagination filled with images of the great Nootka people and their historic meeting with Captain James Cook. It was not hard to imagine the HMS Resolution and HMS Discovery visiting Friendly Cove where the shores were lined with graying cedar-planked houses following the contour of the cove a few metres above the shore. Cook and the great chief Maquinna met in this very location to discuss trading that would long effect the area and now endangered animals like the sea otter.

****

Day 1

What should have been an uneventful three and a half hour drive from Ladysmith to Gold River was lengthened by visits to kayak shops along the way. It was about five hours after leaving Ladysmith that we settled into the Glass Haus, a Bed & Breakfast hosted by Gary and Jeanette Glass. Their gracious and comfortable manner allowed us to relax quickly.

Day 2

After a pancake breakfast the next day we drove 8 miles to where the M.V. Uchuck III docks at the mouth of Gold River. We arrived at 8:00 A.M. on a Saturday, and packed our gear into the kayaks. The recommended time to be ready for the 10:00 A.M. sailing is 8:30 A.M. The crew hoisted our fully loaded boats onto the Uchuck around 9:00 A.M. (Remember to book in advance for passage for you as well as your kayak on the M.V. Uchuck III—phone (250) 283-2515 or http://www.island.net/~mvuchuck/.)

The captain advised us we could be dropped off at Friendly Cove or San Carlos Point on Bligh Island—I'm sure you could negotiate with the captain for another suitable, protected shelter if you had a large party of kayaks. Leaving Gold River, our two-hour trip aboard the converted minesweeper followed the more southerly route around Bligh Island, going down Zuciate Channel to Friendly Cove. There were a number of interesting people on board. A tour guide was also on board and gave a narrative about the areas we were passing through, directed our attention to points of interest, and answered questions about local history.

A group of a dozen nurses were also on board taking a trip to visit a doctor at his summer home at Nootka Fish Camp. After dropping off most of the sightseers in Friendly Cove, we traveled through McKay Passage, between Nootka Island and the Saavedra Islands, on the Uchuck III to Nootka, a cove just north of Boca del Inferno. In the meantime, the nurses had put on white Tyvek overalls with a humorous inscription painted on their backs. After docking the sling hoisted the first group of nurses successfully to the old dock (which still supported an original tin building from the old cannery). The nurses were all giggling and blowing a moose call horn. The sling operator humorously lowered the second group, over, and out-of-view on the opposite side of the revamped minesweeper until the wooden pallet they were standing on started sinking into the water. After several laughs from the remaining crew and passengers on board, the nurses were hoisted back up, across the boat and lowered onto the dock.

That fun set the tone for our trip. After a short crossing of the channel to a logging camp just south of San Carlos Point on Bligh Island we were about to be lowered off the Uchuck into the waters by a sling. The crew placed my kayak on the sling which is a wooden pallet with padded wire rope secured to the four corners and rigged overhead to the freight booms. I put on my sprayskirt and PFD, got into the kayak, put the sprayskirt over the coaming and became airborne. The operator, standing on the forward deck, lifts or lowers kayaks through a unique pulley and sling system up, sideways and then down into the water. The ride was very stable and once in the water a quick stroke of my paddle had me off the pallet.

Gary asked a logger on the nearby dock about bears as he prepared for his sling ride. The logger remarked that he hadn't seen any on Bligh Island though there were wolves.

We settled into the dark, deep green waters and quickly cut through the light chop. We followed the coastline for several kilometres toward the Spanish Pilot Group and Charlie's Beach on the far tip of Bligh Island.

Charlie's Beach is slightly obscured by a rock outcropping. With some maneuvering around rocks you can land in the small cove or paddle around the small point and land on a quarter-moon shaped pebble beach. Charlie's Beach has lots of area for camping and an outhouse! There's a clearing midway between the cove and the pebble beach that offers adequate tent space. There are also 2 or 3 single tent sites just above high water mark on the beach. If you want to avoid some of the mosquitoes camp at one of the higher level spots. There are a variety of locations to choose from. If you find this location crowded, there's another campsite on Vernaci Island directly across from Charlie's Beach. A deserted semi-circular roofed building covered with an orange tarp and cedar needles lies in the forest nearby. Although it's old and musty, it is usable for camping and has a woodstove.

Gary and I were the only campers the first night. We took the opportunity to have a refreshing swim in the ocean, birthday style. Gary took his dip in the cove and I went to the pebble beach. The cove beach is perfect for the evening and the pebble beach awakens idyllically to the morning sun. As it was midday both beaches had sun and the shallow water was warm.

The camp at Charlie's is quite protected from wind. In Nootka Sound and area we found the winds blew from as early as 10:00 A.M. to late afternoon or early evening. We often try to make our greatest distance during windless periods of the day. Being 'Easykayakers' we like to optimize our efforts and maximize our relaxing time. (Some of the wind is due to the uneven warming of land and water. Land typically heats quicker than a large body of water and the air flows out in the mornings. As the water heats up and builds a high-pressure area, the air flows toward the land in the evening.)

Day 3

The next day Gary and I set out on a tour of the islands and coastline. We paddled between Clotchman Island and Narvaez Island in a light breeze. We continued our paddling across a narrow channel to Spouter Island. I was finding the scenery in this area much more spectacular than the coast of Bligh Island. Gentle swells pushed us along the southeast shore of Spouter.

The east coast of Spouter Island is part of Ewin Inlet. Careful planning has to be made before paddling the full length of the inlet and back (approx. 7 km). You can be fooled into a leisurely paddle to the cove at the end of the inlet only to face strong wind and waves on the way out. Gary observed from the Uchuck III how the weather and huge, West Coast rollers funneled mid-afternoon into Ewin Inlet on our trip to Friendly Cove. (We had planned a third day into the inlet but as you will see in this journal, gale force winds were in the works.)

A tent was perched on a rock outcropping separated by a very narrow strip of sea off the northern tip of Spouter Island and near Bligh Island. We were quite awed that someone would even consider placing a tent here. I circumnavigated the tiny isle and found no launch sites. A small rope was hung between the isle and Bligh Island so we guessed a powerboat tied and anchored here and the campers would then have climbed to their solitary perch.

The inlet west of Ewin Inlet (Tuttle Cove) is the home of Sunkissed Fishing Lodge. The owners graciously keep fresh water on deck for kayakers. We chatted with them for several minutes discussing B.C. politics

(Glen Clark had just resigned). After exploring Tuttle Cove we alighted at a campsite just out of view of the floating lodge. We explored the site. It's quite usable but definitely a second choice for camping. We much preferred Charlie's Beach, which is where we headed for a late lunch.

After eating, reading, swimming, snacking and reading again, the midday winds abated so we launched our kayaks to explore the Vernaci Island campsite and to leisurely circumnavigate Verdia Island. Evening paddles are often the most picturesque and enlightening times. The sun set perfectly that evening over the Spanish Pilot Group while we were finishing our supper back at Charlie's Beach.

Day 4

The next morning after listening to the weather channel we made a difficult decision. We had planned to explore Ewin Inlet in the early morning, but after listening to our weather radio we made a snap decision to head for Friendly Cove. A gale force wind for north Vancouver Island was in the works. A front was moving in. Would it affect Nootka Sound? We decided to pack up camp.

The morning was quite hilarious. We moved our kayaks to where we thought it would be a safe distance from the incoming tide. However, about halfway into our packing, the tide was touching our sterns. We hastily finished packing and described it as our worse job ever. Usually we pack our lunch fixings last so they will be easily accessible at the appointed time. Today in our rush, this didn't happen.

We paddled to the tip of Vernaci Island and headed on a west by northwest bearing to a river north of Nootka Fishing Camp on Nootka Island. This was a bit of a detour, but we wanted to have a look at the coastline. The 2-km crossing was quite uneventful. We had very gentle glassy rolling swells and no wind. The sky was blue and it seemed a perfect day for paddling. In hindsight I think we had visions of gale force winds striking us in mid-channel; our imagination was working a little too well that morning. We are experienced kayakers but we really do enjoy casual, dry paddling more than being wind-beaten and ocean-washed.

We pulled into a semi-sandy shore and walked the log-strewn beach to the creek. I picked up an eagle's feather as Gary saw a logging company pickup truck pass only 100 metres away on the hillside. We weren't that far away from fellow man, but if it weren't for seeing the truck, we would have never known that. The north end of Bligh Island also has some on-going logging operations, but it seems well hidden from the park area.

The village of Nootka Fish Camp was our next stop of interest. An original cannery building and dock stood on the south shore of the cove with the fish camp and several dozen homes lining the rest of the shore.

Just beyond the camp we paddled to Boca del Inferno at slack tide, through it, and into a lake-sized lagoon. A large rock affects the tidal flow in and out of the narrow inlet of the Inferno. During a flood or ebb flow a waterfall is created with approximately a two-foot drop. One group of people we met later had experimented at the site. They sent their one plastic kayak into the lagoon. He was pulled through the narrow passage quite quickly and dropped out of sight of the other kayakers when he was sucked over the little waterfall. A short distance later he came back into view. He then realized he couldn't paddle back out until the tide changed. His fellow kayakers fed a line through the Inferno and the 'plastic kayaker' tied it to his craft. He deposited himself on shore to hike across a point of land while the other kayakers easily pulled the plastic kayak up the waterfall and through the narrow inlet. There's all sorts of fun kayaking!

The winds came up as we left Boca Del Inferno Bay and headed into McKay Passage. The Saavedra Islands chain probably gave us some protection, but it didn't feel like it. We were faced with three kilometres of windy paddling. About a kilometre before Friendly Cover we hit the sheltered waters of Santa Gertrudis Cove. By this time our stomachs were telling us that it was past lunch time.

Santa Gertrudis Cove was a welcome spot for a rest. We checked out all four sandy beaches for campsites but found none above the high tide line. It took a little digging and repacking to find our lunch goodies. We could hear the wind roar high over our heads and after a leisurely lunch, we bit the bullet and headed out into the wind for the final leg into Friendly Cove.

That last kilometre was a real snort. We tightened our hatbands and pulled the bills low so they wouldn't blow off. Our paddles felt like they weighed 10 pounds due to wind resistance. Gary's kayak was highly waxed and kept pulling ahead even though he seemed to be paddling slower. We arrived in Friendly Cove and set up tent by a wooden shelter in the large field. This proved to be a fortunate decision, as within a short time we would experience hours of wind-driven rain pelting down on our tents.

After supper the winds seemed to stop as they had each day before. Around midnight the wind rose again and the rain began, the storm front had reached us at Friendly Cove. The foghorn began sounding and continued throughout the night as the winds began to sweep the shores and the waves pounded the singing pebble beaches.

****

Friendly Cove (Yuguot) resides on the southeast corner of Nootka Island. Over 4,000 Nuu-chah-nulth once lived at Yuquot (place of many winds).

The Mowachaht chief of Yuquot, Maquinna, met Captain James Cook here. It is said to be where the First Nations people of British Columbia first discovered Europeans in their midst. The site is now designated as a National Historic Site by the Canadian government. Friendly Cove is also the only location the Spanish have tried to settle in Canada. The place is steeped in First Nations and European history.

The present church was built in 1956. It replaced a church that burned down in 1954. When you first walk up the stairs and through the arched doorway you expect to see a hall filled with rows of oak wooden pews separated by an aisle leading to the altar. But the church is a museum for unique replicas of traditional native interior houseposts. Much like totem poles, they were put inside Mowachaht houses instead of outside. One of the pieces hanging over the entrance is a huge eagle; underneath on the floor is a killer whale carving.

The lighthouse is now in the location of the once Spanish fort. Two families of keepers maintain the operation of the lighthouse in 12 hour back-to-back shifts of 2 weeks. The buildings and grounds are impeccably kept.

****

Day 5

After a breakfast of porridge and hot chocolate, and dressed in excellent raingear, Gary and I set out for the 3½ hour hike along the shoreline. On this hike and when kayaking across from Burdwood Point (a campsite) you might see whales that occasionally frequent these waters and shoreline. The trail passes along a modern graveyard (early 1900s to 1960s) and past a large freshwater lake to a series of six cabins that are for rent by the Mowachaht/Muchalaht First Nations Band office in Gold River (phone 250-283-2015).

The walkway to the cabins is quite well maintained. Past the cabins, veer right onto a trail just as the walkway reaches the beach. The trail is marked by typical 2 metre high salal and largely parallels the coastline. To walk to the lagoon outflow, enter the beach near a large rock wall and outcropping. Follow the beach to the lagoon. You can pick up a brochure while you're sailing on the Uchuck that shows these Yatz-mahs trail locations. The brochure is also available at the Band office in Gold River.

You can camp in the upper high tide zone near the lagoon. The land in this area is privately owned and must be respected. It is fairly difficult to land on the steep beaches. You can paddle into the outflow of the lagoon for a few yards and then pull up your kayaks more easily.

We ate our lunch sheltered from the wind near the lagoon in the drizzle and made our way back to camp with cold wet feet (we had runners not hiking boots). By late afternoon the winds had picked up significantly. I was beginning to get moisture in my tent and worried slightly that I would soon be coping with a wet sleeping bag. I knew I needed to scotchguard my fly better next trip and seamguard the zipper and seams.

During the night (Tuesday) the winds had increased to 80 km/hr. Gary and I had anchored our tents well. We stayed inside our sleeping bags and read our books waiting out the storm. Gary had been listening to the weather news when it was interrupted with a report—a Russian MIG-21 jet on a training mission with the HMCS Algonquin had crashed off Estevan Point south of Friendly Cove. The next morning several helicopters including Search and Rescue flew overhead searching for the missing pilot and plane. He had unfortunately died in the crash. The Coast Guard described the conditions as terrible. We concurred with this weather report.

Day 6

Wednesday morning was bright and beautiful. I was running out of dry clothes and really appreciated the summer sun. We had been the only kayakers at Friendly cove until mid-morning when small groups started arriving. By now we had our boats loaded so we went for a short paddle around Friendly Cove and then returned to the beach to join several storm wearied kayakers ready to take the Uchuck III back home. More kayakers arrived and we all swapped stories and had lunch together. Most had been quite anxious about the weather in the morning. Two women had set out from Burdwood Point campsite in reasonable weather. However, the remnants of the gale had whipped up the waters for the last half of their crossing of Nootka Sound. They seemed quite glad to have their feet anchored in the warm pebbles of Friendly Cove.

The conditions can change dramatically during a crossing. While you may not need a VHF radio for some kayak expeditions, trips open to the Pacific Ocean warrant the expenditure! Proper equipment is essential to kayaking in these waters.

We were spirited onto the Uchuck III around 1:00 P.M. and left port around 2:15 P.M. Heather Harbord, author of *Nootka Sound*, had been on board the day before. Gary purchased a copy of her book. We recommend her book to anyone exploring this area. Along the cruise back, we observed much of the coastline with binoculars and snapped a few pictures. The Uchuck stopped at Resolution Cove. Captain Cook had spent a month in 1778 here. Two plaques commemorating the event are imbedded on the shoreline and are easily seen from the ship. We arrived in Gold River around 4:30 P.M. The crew quickly unloaded our boats onto the dock ending our kayaking adventure of Nootka Sound.

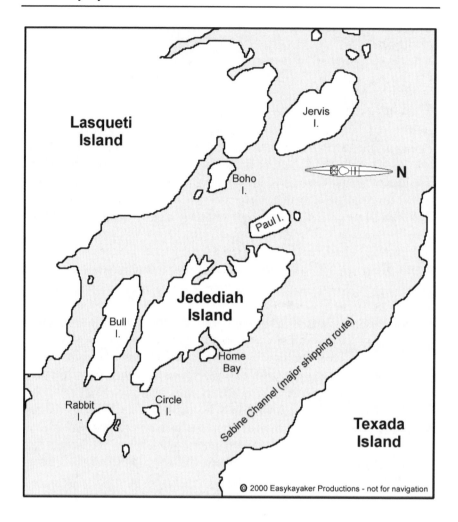

Chart #3512
Tidal Reference: Point Atkinson

Jedediah's horse "Will" at age 30

Jedediah Island

It all started with a newspaper article in the Nanaimo paper about an island that was becoming a BC Marine Park. The entire island 243 ha. (600 acres) was owned by one family and was being sold to the BC government for a park at roughly half its value. I kept this article in my kayaking drawer of the family filing cabinet (it's now grown to two drawers) and I would come across it every once in a while when digging for something.

The idea of a kayak camping trip on the island really appealed to me and one night, while surfing the web, I found an informative article written by Bob Schroeder on the Wave~Length website about Jedediah and how to get there. But how to get there wasn't easy and that was a problem. Consequently, the trip got postponed again.

About a year later the Nanaimo newspaper carried another story about Jedediah Island. This time the article mentioned that a book had been written about it. Mary Palmer, the island's last owner and person most responsible for it becoming a park, had just had her book *Jedediah Days* published (ISBN 1-55017-184-4). Fortunately the Vancouver Island Regional Library purchased a few copies and I was able to check one out within a few days.

The book was both enjoyable and informative, but more than anything else, it cemented in my mind the desire to visit the island. But getting there was still a problem. We could paddle there or take a charter or, or, or… There were a lot of possibilities but none sounded great.

One route was to paddle from Schooner Cove to the Ballenas Islands and then make the 10 km crossing to Lasqueti Island and over to Jedediah (24 km total distance). Another way was to take the private ferry to Lasqueti and paddle around Lasqueti Island to Jedediah Island (20 km trip). The easiest way would be to drive to Comox, take the ferry to Powell River, take a ferry from Powell River to Texada Island, drive across Texada and paddle about 8 km to Jedediah's Home Bay. The last option open to us was to charter a boat that would drop us on Jedediah with our boats and gear.

As this was to be a family trip, paddling a long distance was out. The driving and ferry route was too time-consuming and too expensive considering that we would be trailering the kayaks. So chartering a boat seemed like the best option. Naturally, our costs would be lower if we could find a few fellow kayakers to join us and share the cost.

Booking the charter was easy. I did a few searches on the Internet and came up with four companies that offered charters to Jedediah. Of the four, I was most impressed with Cliff Hermann's Seadog Sailing & Kayaking. Trying to find fellow kayakers to fit our trip schedule was more difficult and in the end it turned into a family-only adventure, which was nice for the three of us.

Now the problem of taking a charter right to our destination was that we weren't limited to only the amount of gear that would fit into our kayaks so we packed way too much. This became apparent when the time came to load everything into the large beautiful sailboat that was a long walk down the docks. How three people could fill up five large wheelbarrows (standard dockside mode of transportation) with food and gear for only five days, I'm not sure, but we were headed for luxury camping and gourmet dining from the looks of things.

The 24 km sailing trip to Jedediah was a relaxing scenic voyage on a warm early summer day. About halfway there we gave up on the wind and started the motor again. Cliff pointed out the landmarks and islands plus gave us a bit of history and a who's-who of the owners of the different islands. Katherine at age 12 got a lesson on how to pilot the sailboat by dead reckoning and by compass. She piloted the boat for much of the voyage while Cliff did some minor maintenance and stowing of gear. Teesh and I sat back and enjoyed the views.

We planned to camp at Home Bay and therefore timed our arrival for high tide. Home Bay has the only natural sandy beach for miles around but all of Home Bay becomes dry at low tide. Because Home Bay isn't very deep and has a reef near the entrance, Cliff moored the sailboat in the next cove to the south, Codfish Bay. We loaded half of our gear into Cliff's inflatable dinghy, climbed into our kayaks and headed off. The kayaks beat Cliff's motorized dinghy to the campsite but only because we had a head start. It took two dingy trips to unload all the gear, but soon Cliff was on his way home and we were setting up camp.

There were two other people already camping on Jedediah but with 600 acres we managed to find room. The other two were out fishing by kayak when we arrived, so we didn't get to meet them until around suppertime. It turned out that both were on what I would consider epic kayak trips. Steve, on his two-week holiday from work, was on his way from Vancouver to Hornby Island in a used plastic kayak without a rudder. The almost 100 km journey was just about over and he would soon be meeting up with his family on Hornby Island in a day or two.

Brian, the other kayaker, and Steve had just met. Brian had started from Anacortes, Washington and was planning to paddle about 1000 km to Prince Rupert. He was about 175 km into his trip. Brian's a teacher from California and a very experienced kayaker.

Our first supper was half cooked when our very dependable one-burner stove ran out of fuel. Normally I top up the fuel and check out the stove at home before a trip, but for some reason I didn't this time. Not only was it out of fuel, but we couldn't open the filler cap as it had become slightly corroded. That'll teach me, practice what you preach!

Within two minutes we had a cooking fire going in the park's fire pit on the beach and as an added benefit we were able to enjoy sitting around the fire after supper. For desert Teesh had made and brought some wonderful almond squares that we shared with Steve and Brian. As the summer solstice had been only a few weeks before, it stayed light until almost bedtime.

The weather had been good and there was no rain predicted for the next few days, but gale force winds came up overnight. Our tent was exposed and the top danced a bit. When morning of day 2 arrived the winds continued. Steve and Brian packed up and left, but said if it was too rough on the outside that they would return.

After breakfast, we took off to explore Jedediah. It was a beautiful, warm summer day out of the wind. We headed across Home Bay, which was now dry due to low tide, we beachcombed and explored tide pools. Once across Home Bay we explored the old homestead and sheds, and read the plaques. One of the plaques was a memorial to Dan Culver, an accomplished world adventurer and environmentalist. In 1993 Dan and Jim Haberl were the first Canadians to reach the summit of K-2, the world's highest peak. On the way down Dan fell to his death. Dan's will directed that his estate go to preserving a wilderness area on the BC Coast. His posthumous gift of $1.1 million helped raise the $4.2 million needed to buy Jedediah. We found out later that Dan was friends with a friend of ours (it's a small world and Vancouver Island is a small island). After reflecting on Dan's gift we headed off on our hike to Deep Bay. Mary Palmer's book contains a map of all the coves, bays, trails and points of interest, which we brought along and used for our land navigation.

Jedediah is a hiker's paradise. Goats are believed to have been left on the island about 200 years ago by the Spanish explorers. Goats along with the Palmer's sheep and horse "Will" keep a network of trails open and well grazed. The main trails are old narrow tractor roads that wind through fields and forests of large trees. Everywhere we went, large rock outcroppings offered Katherine many climbing opportunities. At Deep Bay we enjoyed the views of Paul and Lasqueti Islands.

On the way back to camp we knew Home Bay would be flooded, so we took the land route to our camp. Back at camp we had a late lunch and saw that Brian had returned. Brian had paddled up to the north end of Texada Island and decided to forgo the long crossing until the winds subsided. After a short visit with Brian we decided to spend a lazy afternoon reading and relaxing. Brian joined us for a supper of spatzel and Greek salad and then a game of catch with the foxtail.

Day 3 was another windy day, so we decided that after a late breakfast we would hike up Mount Gibraltar, which at an elevation of 478 feet, is the highest point on Jedediah. We had read about the jar in the rock cairn at Gibraltar's summit. Visitors have left notes in a jar there for over 100 years.

Brian decided to stay another day due to wind and headed up Mount Gibraltar ahead of us. Shortly after he left, Will the horse came walking over across the mudflats of Home Bay. Many signs warn against feeding Will as he will become quite aggressive. Will is a 30-year-old horse that has learned a thing or two in life and certainly knows his mind.

Will invaded Brian's unguarded campsite looking for food and was threatening to step on or fertilize Brian's paddle and other gear. We herded Will out of Brian's camp and moved a few of his things to a safer location. Teesh being a horse person in her younger days took a couple of sticks and curried Will, which he appeared to thoroughly enjoy. She examined his hooves and commented that someone must visit regularly to care for him. Will was putty in her hands and she was able to control him quite well, but heeded the warnings and did not attempt to mount him. A day later Katherine and I met five hikers from a sailboat who hadn't read the warning signs and had been terrorized by Will. I'm not a horse person and did find myself later (without Teesh) in the middle of a field with a rapidly approaching Will. Once he realized that my camera and Katherine's Frisbee weren't edible, he lost interest and left.

Breakfast dishes done, we headed off toward Long Bay to find the trail up Gibraltar. Mary Palmer's map showed where the trail to Gibraltar forked off from the main trail that leads to Long Bay. When we reached Long Bay, we knew we had missed the trail. Near Long Bay are open fields and on the eastside of the fields is where the trail forked off from the main trail. This is not where the map shows it starting, so we followed the map and with compass in hand, charged up a series of goat trails until we spotted some flagging and found the right trail. The right trail was not much better than the goat trails but the flagging was enough to let us know that we were on the right track, although occasionally we needed to backtrack and hunt for flagging. This became part of the game and it was an enjoyable hike to the top and what a breathtaking view we found.

The jar was in the cairn and we carefully removed the notes and read them. Earlier notes have been archived and the oldest one remaining was about 25 years old. There was a pencil in the jar, so we each added a note as had Brian before us. Teesh being a secretary rearranged all of the notes in chronological order.

There are different views from different areas up top of Gibraltar so we hiked around exploring and enjoying the area. One viewscape was Home Bay looking very small and distant. On our hike down we followed the trail and found where it starts at the field. I'm sure when Mary drew her map, the trail started in a different spot, but trails have a way of changing over time.

Brian was at camp reading when we had our late lunch. It was still windy in exposed areas, but Home Bay was flooded so Brian and I paddled around it after lunch while Katherine played on a raft that she had made from rope, styrofoam blocks and driftwood that she had found. After our short paddle Brian gave us a hand relocating our camp from prime Home Bay beachfront to a sheltered forest location near Codfish Bay. After two windy nights of sleeping in a dancing tent, it was time for a change of pace. I did an assessment of the trees in the area to make sure that we weren't going to a site that would be dangerous. Of course as soon as we moved camp, the weather changed and the wind began to decrease.

Brian had mailed supplies and charts to post offices up the coast, but he was now behind schedule. We lent him our cellular phone to call Alert Bay so he could confirm with the post office there that he was on his way and for them to please hold his package. The post office had the package and would continue to hold it. They also had a message from his wife that they passed on to him. Small town service is second to none. As weather conditions were improving, this would be his last night on Jedediah, so we had a final supper together and gave him some of our extra water.

Day 4 started very early for us with a momma goat on a ridge on one side of our tent and baby goat on the other. It couldn't have been much past dawn when the noise started. Having raised many generations of goats I claim to understand goat talk to a certain degree. The young goat said "Baaaaaaa," which meant "let's go this way." Momma in a deeper tone said "Baaaaa," which meant, "No, we're going this way. Come over here at once." The young one said, "No I can't, I'm scared, there's a tent in the way." The mother replied, "That's nonsense, come this way now!" This is a very condensed version of the conversation that continued way too long with neither side budging (goats can be stubborn). I finally got up, went out of the tent and settled the debate for the moment. I don't think either Momma or her young'un were happy to see me, but they forgot their differences and hurried off together.

After breakfast, Katherine and I went for a hike and then all three of us went for a nice paddle. The main reason for the paddle was to move the boats from Home Bay to Codfish Bay. We did some fun exploring. The sheer rock faces had some very interesting and colourful marine life for us to examine. We paddled past Codfish Bay at a very leisurely pace, exploring every reef and crevice. Part way to Little Bull Passage Teesh decided we should turn back to Codfish Bay. I wasn't ready to stop paddling, so once back at Codfish I picked up my fishing gear and went back out. If there were any codfish in Codfish Bay, they didn't fall for my fishing techniques.

While I was fishing Katherine met our early morning goat friends. Mom and dad goat gave her a wide berth but of course the young goat was curious (kids will be kids). Katherine got a good picture of the baby goat hanging over the ledge looking down at her from nearby. Naturally momma goat wasn't happy and more "Baaaaas" were exchanged. After the goats, Katherine climbed the huge rocks alongside Codfish Bay and got a good photo of me in the kayak about 75 feet below her.

Day 5 started with us breaking camp and carrying everything to the beach at Codfish Bay in preparation for being picked up by Cliff Hermann and his sailboat. We did this quick enough to allow me to go for a solo kayak paddle into Little Bull Passage. I explored every beach on the way, getting out of the kayak and beachcombing through the large piles of driftwood. Just after getting back into my boat after one of these beach explorations I saw a family of otters climbing about 30 feet up a hillside. As soon as I spotted them I froze, but it was too late, they had seen me and reversed their direction back toward the water. Watching them come down the hillside was impressive. They moved fast on the steep slope and dove from quite high.

Little Bull Passage is a beautiful place to paddle, however the wind was rising and Cliff would soon be arriving. Reluctantly I headed back to Codfish Bay and arrived shortly before Cliff did. Loading our gear onto the sailboat went quickly, we said goodbye to Jedediah Island with hopes of returning someday soon.

The sailboat ride back was great. It was a day made for sailing with blue skies and steady wind. The waves were hitting our port side dead on and the boat rolled gracefully with each one. The wind was strong enough that we had only one sail up and even that one was reefed in a bit. It was definitely an exciting and fast ride back to Schooner Cove. As we neared the entrance to the cove, we slowed to allow a group of kayakers to pull into the cove ahead of us. Cliff explained that they were a youth group that his guides had taken on a short overnight trip to a nearby island.

Our family certainly recommends Jedediah Island as a great place to visit. Although it has been "discovered", there's plenty of elbow room and many great areas to camp. The outhouses are nice and well maintained, but there is no drinking water available, so bring your own. There are marshy areas near Home Bay, but we were surprised by how few mosquitoes there were considering the time of year.

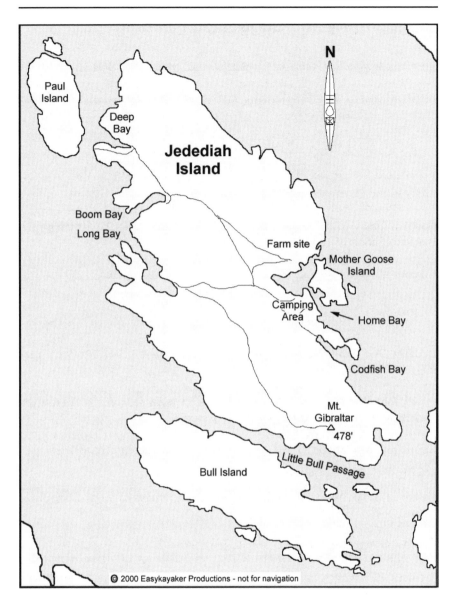

We hope you have found *Easykayaker—the book* useful and fun to read. Happy Paddling!

Gary Backlund
Paul Grey

Bibliography and Suggested Reading

Backroad Mapbook, Volume II: Vacouver Island, Mussio Ventures Ltd., 1997

Blades, Michael. *Day of Two Sunsets, Paddling Adventures on Canada's West Coast,* Orca Book Publishers, 1993

BC Marine Parks Guide, OP Publishing Ltd., 1999

Chart 1—Symbols, Abbreviations and Terms, Canadian Hydrographic Service, Fisheries and Oceans Canada, 1996

Colbeck, Lynda A. *Vancouver Island Shores, seashore exploring for the novice,* Protected Shores of Vancouver Island, 1998

Cummings, Al. *Gunkholing in the Gulf Islands,* Nor'westing, Inc., 1989

Current Atlas—Juan de Fuca to Strait of Georgia, ISBN 0-660-52380-9, produced by the Canadian Hydrographic Service, Department of Fisheries and Oceans

Douglas, Don. *Exploring Vancouver Island's West Coast, a Cruising Guide, Fine Edge Productions,* 1994

Dowd, John. *Sea Kayaking,* Greystone Books, Douglas & McIntyre, Vancouver/ Toronto. University of Washington Press, Seattle, 1997

Environment Canada, 1998 http://www.cmc.ec.gc.ca/climate/normals/ E_BC_WMO.HTM

Harbord, Heather. *Nootka Sound and the Surrounding Waters of Maquinna,* Heritage House, 1996

Henderson, V.I. *Piper's Lagoon,* Henderson, 1984

Merilees, Bill. *Newcastle Island, a Place of Discovery – A Place of Discovery,* Heritage House, 1998

Kayak Routes of the Pacific NorthWest Coast, edited by Peter McGee, Greystone Books, 1998

Palmer, Mary. *Jedediah Days,* Harbour Publishing, 1998

Snowden, Mary Ann. *Island Paddling.* Orca Book Publishers, 1997

Wave~Length Paddling Magazine, edited by Alan Wilson, issues from April 1997 to January 2001

Index